T0208051

Worshipping
Christ Jesus to Usher
in the New Millennium

Worshipping Christ Jesus to Usher in the New Millennium

Withstanding in the Second Heaven in The End Times

MISS DESTINY AND PURPOSE

WORSHIPPING CHRIST JESUS TO USHER IN THE NEW MILLENNIUM
Withstanding in the Second Heaven in The End Times

iUniverse books may be ordered through booksellers or by contacting:

iUniverse
1663 Liberty Drive
Bloomington, IN 47403
www.iuniverse.com
1-800-Authors (1-800-288-4677)

ISBN: 978-1-4917-7218-8 (sc)
ISBN: 978-1-4917-7217-1 (e)

Library of Congress Control Number: 2015911263

Print information available on the last page.

iUniverse rev. date: 07/15/2015

Contents

Dedication

Firstly to the object, subject and purpose of all my praise and worship, the only One we should worship, the Almighty God in flesh—the Lord Jesus Christ. You are So Wonderful, my heart sings for joy unspeakable and full of Glory.

To the human heart that really wants to press through to find the fulfillment, joy and satisfaction of being in God's presence. This is for those who want to seek His face and not just His Hand for a blessing. It is for those who desire to be conformed into His image and likeness.

To all believers who desire the "above only life under an open heaven" in their daily lives and to see the reality of God's presence in the world of family, the world of work, and the world of life.

To my late mother, Mrs Mary Norma De Weever Small who as a stalwart of the medical profession (she was asked three times to be the Matron of the Georgetown Public Hospital Guyana but she graciously declined to care more for her family). Her godly life and example and dedication to the health and wellbeing of her family and country will forever be our divine family legacy and hope. She is now worshipping Him among the heavenly hosts of witnesses.

To my father and siblings who are now getting on board in the deeper life work of the Holy Spirit. Keep on seeking

His Face and you will never regret the quality time spent in His presence.

To the late Sister Doris Nurse who always encouraged me –To get in with the Lord (this was her way of saying to get closer to the Lord) She would also say-"This is it" (we always wondered what she was talking about until we pressed on in our Christian walk and discovered the "it' being a fresh revelation of the Lord Jesus Christ. Well my dear Sister Nurse this book is a legacy of your encouragement.

To Dr. Judson Cornwall, who devoted so much of his writing to Praise and Worship that this is living proof of his own experience with the Lord. His book—Worship as Jesus Taught It- was particularly useful in enhancing my own worship experience with the Lord.

Preface

Worship for the Christian is the highest level of spiritual warfare. It shows who we worship as our God and distinguishes us as separate and distinct because all other worship of any other god is idolatry which is subject to complete defeat. So, we are not in competition with other religions neither are we complimenting them. Like Moses and Elijah who were transfigured on the Mount of Transfiguration we as believers are called to high level worship in the heavenlies. Likewise like the Apostle Paul we have to be caught up to the third heaven and by revelations gained from there carry out our assignments more effectively.

The Early Church was established by so great an outpouring of the Holy Spirit on the Day Of Pentecost that the place they were in in the Upper Room shook as with a mighty wind. Those gathered there were never the same. They were equipped to go into all the world and preach the Gospel. The Power of the Holy Spirit is indeed awesome to empower the saints that all opposition to God's move is crushed.

The realm of the Zodiac and astrology are more active in negatively influencing the work of the Church of Jesus Christ than many believers can imagine. This is because of the high level of deception that is being employed by the kingdom of darkness. However, as Jesus promised—he will build His Church and the gates of hell shall not prevail against it. God will always ensure that the necessary knowledge and other equipping of His is given to His people.

One of the great blessings of truth is that it not only sets us free but makes us free as well. It is hoped that the research given here will prove life changing and transform our worship experience significantly.

Miss Destiny And Purpose
Brooklyn, New York
2015

Acknowledgements

This work is the product of many years as a child of God sitting at the feet of the Lord Jesus Christ the True Rabbi of my faith. This has taught me how to love Him so very much.

I am also very grateful to many great men and women of God from various ministries who do not know how much their devotion to true and pure worship has impacted my life. I either visited their ministries briefly on special occasions when invited by friends, by listening to worship CDS and by observing them on television from time to time. Don Moen, Integrity Music Team, Darlene Zich, Charlene Davis of Jamaica, the Daystar singers, Dave and Margarit Hinds of Youth with a Mission are just a mere few of the numerous examples I can cite.

To the many prayer teams of various ministries who always have a sweet worship atmosphere during prayer times in radio and TV land.

Thank you all so very very much.

Introduction

As a believer myself of over twenty five years I have always been drawn to the topic of true worship and spiritual warfare. My pursuit of this interest always yielded the greatest breakthroughs in my personal walk with the Lord Jesus Christ. I know I am not the only Christian with this victory report and while countless Christians have written and published thousands of books on this topic this is my very first attempt at writing and publishing a book. My target audience therefore is the 'born again Christian' in what is widely known as the Body of Christ. I would therefore use terminologies such as we, our and you interchangeably as this is how all Christians are seen by God; as one corporate united body or family.

We are called as the Body of Christ to be changed from glory to glory and to be conformed into Christ image and likeness. This is imperative as we prepare as His Bride for His Return to earth and His Glorious Reign on earth referred to as the Millennium. All this can only be accomplished by effective worship and warfare especially in the Second Heaven. This is worship and warfare at its very zenith as we lift our eyes and hearts to the skies looking for His Glorious Appearing. It is the culmination of all spiritual battles of all the Ages. It is therefore the season of transformational worship as we are changed into His likeness and image.

We as believers know the Word of God as it relates to all areas of life such as worship and spiritual warfare. The Book of Ephesians chapter 6 explains fully about who and or what we are fighting against and the nature of the armor that all Christians must wear or put on as the bible admonishes us to do. We are called to worship Jesus Christ and commissioned by Him to war aggressively against these evil spiritual hosts in the spirit realm. We are to war valiantly, without compromise showing no mercy to satan and the kingdom of darkness. The greatest resistance we will encounter is in the Second Heaven as we become seated with Christ far above all principality and power. This is why the armor of God is given to us. We now need to know more about these principalities and powers.

This book is published to highlight some insights to worship of God in the heavenlies as it relates to the Body of Christ. It is hoped that we would gain significant progress in understanding how to superimpose God's original plan, will and intent over the Kingdom of darkness as shown in Ephesians chapters 1,2 and 3 KJV. These scriptures clearly state God's manifold wisdom in that – "He hath chosen us in Him before the foundation of the world that we should be holy and without blame before Him in love (Ephesians 1:4' KJV) that in the dispensation of the fullness of times He might gather together in one all things in Christ both which are in heaven and which are on earth, even in Him (Ephesians 1:10 KJV). And to make all men see what is the fellowship of the mystery which from the beginning of the world hath been hid in God who created all things by Jesus Christ----to the intent that now unto the principalities and powers in heavenly places might be known by the church the manifold wisdom of God". According to the eternal purpose which He purposed in Christ Jesus our Lord. In whom we have boldness and access with confidence by the faith of Him (Ephesians 3: 10-12. KJV)

How much we value something will determine how much we are willing to pay for it. Since mankind is made in the image and likeness of God our value is so high that God paid the highest price for our redemption by sending Jesus to die for our sins. So Jesus did not die to improve our value but to redeem it. It is only in Him that we recognize who and whose we are. We must come back to our Creator to appropriate this glorious treasure. That is why being independent of God is dangerous. We can never know our value outside of God. It's the main weapon in the hand of the Spirit of Pride and Rebellion that characterizes the fallen angel Lucifer who is now satan.

Now praising and worshipping God in Spirit and in truth necessitates of course the full and constant outworking of the finished work of Jesus on the Cross. Thus we would return to God's original purpose will and intent for redeemed mankind---to bear Christ image and reign and rule effectively over the principalities and powers and rulers of darkness etc of Ephesians 6: 12- 18 KJV. Always keep in mind the following:

a) Jesus Christ is the one God used to create all things including Lucifer (Ephesians 3:9, KJV Colossians 1:16. KJV) Lucifer could never be God as he himself is a created creature.

b) Jesus Christ is the Head of all principality and power and uses all created things whether thrones, powers or principalities to accomplish His will (Colossians 2:9, 10 Philippians 2: 9-11 KJV)

c) Jesus Christ is God (I and the Father are one, whoever sees Me sees the Father also)

d) Lucifer and the principalities and powers worshipped Jesus Christ as God in heaven before they fell.

e) Lucifer is the first one to deceive mankind about the Trinity of God—he made three separate gods. It's one God we serve in three different offices but it is still one God—the Lord Jesus Christ. These three different Gods distort our concept of God and ultimately our worship of Him.

It is a proven fact that whoever or whatever we focus on, dwell on, and consumes all our energy—that thing or person is in essence our God. You will ultimately produce after its kind. You will be changed, transfigured and metamorphosed accordingly. Man in his fallen state cannot worship God effectively and certainly cannot have God's image. A way had to be found to remedy this disconnect between God and man. Praise God Jesus Christ healed this breach and reconnected us back to God. The earth now that was groaning to see the manifestation of the sons of God can now witness that awesome miracle through the Body of Christ in full worship transformation being just as Christ is in heaven. Imagine the earth filled with people looking just like Christ. This is why had the principalities and powers known that Christ death would have caused their total defeat and immobilization, they would not have crucified Him (1 Corinthians2: 7-8 KJV). Jesus mission to earth was pre-planned and ordained before the foundation of the earth. He accomplished it perfectly and completely on the Cross. This is why the first thing He did after His resurrection was to gather and commission His disciples to go into all the world and preach the Gospel of the Kingdom of God baptizing all men, nations and races teaching them all things I have taught you, Mark 16;15 KJV. This would eventually change all men into the image and likeness of God.

The plan of the enemy who is raging mad at what Jesus death had accomplished and knowing his time is short, is fighting full force against the true worship of Jesus Christ in the Church. He knows that God inhabits the praises of His people to the extent we can and will be transfigured/metamorphosed into His glorious image and be at His throne constantly. God can do wonders with our worship as happened with the Apostle Paul (2 Corinthians 12:3-4 KJV) Paul and Silas sang praises unto God in the Roman jail and an earthquake shook the prison doors open, but amazingly the prisoners did not make a run for their freedom but rather remained and experienced a life changing moment. The jailer got afraid and asked—"What must I do to be saved?"

When the Body of Christ praises God it produces results such as these:

a) It causes shifts in the heavenlies and brings down satanic strongholds such as pride, rebellion, murder, witchcraft etc.

b) It routs, disturbs and ultimately immobilizes the Kingdom of Darkness.

c) It gives God the legal right to operate in a body—the Body of Christ on the earth.

d) We the Body of Christ are changed from glory to glory.

e) The six levels of the operation of the Holy Spirit are in full force (Dunamis, Excousia, Arche, Kratos, Ischus, Prata) as signs and wonders follow. Dunamis is miracle working power, Excousia is delegated power, Ischus is great strong power, Kratos is dominion and raw power, Arche is first or authoritative power, Prata is resurrection power.

f) The Body of Christ bears Christ image more and more as we are metamorphosed.

g) We are more useful in God's hands as we are metamorphosed and we can now superimpose God's Word, Law, Rule and Authority over the Kingdom of Darkness.

The worship experience of Christ Church on earth must enter the realm of the theophanic. This is what happened when Jesus was metamorphosed on the Mount of Transfiguration. We must attain this revelatory dimension by seeking God with all our hearts, souls and the renewing of our minds. This is why the ritual of a typical man-made service on a Sunday morning must change. It typically runs like this; 'First we'll have a hymn (a hymn is chosen) Now we'll read the scripture text from(scriptures are chosen) then we'll have two more hymns. We'll now have a time of worship and then our preacher will bring the Word. Are there any new- comers –raise your hands. Are there any birthdays? Now we'll have the announcements and the offering. The benediction is then read and the service is ended by man.

From what was said in the first few paragraphs above about the necessity to have a proper knowledge of the assignment of the principalities and powers and to put on the whole armor of God, this typical church service routine has to be taken over by the Spirit of the Lord completely.

Some churches are waking up to the fact that the intercessors, prayer and worship leaders must be truly purified, pray and fast days before and 'pray up' the service. These services will have a freshness the others lack. Then the pastor says "let us wait on the Lord and hear what He wants today. Hallelujah! Mighty breakthroughs occur at these services as man-made programs are completely forgotten in the wonder of seeing the moving of God's Holy Spirit. It's all about worship, it's all about worship, it's all about worship. The true worshipper becomes the true warrior. We must bring every thought into captivity to the obedience of Christ as we renew our minds and have the mind of Christ. If you don't worship you cannot do warfare.

Finally, we can know more about the specific assignment of each principality and power as stated in Ephesians 6. JP Timmons through his own personal experiences as a missionary in Nigeria, Africa for over twenty five years gives a most insightful revelation in his book----"Mysterious Secrets of the Kingdom of Darkness---the battle for planet earth". Likewise, Amanda Buys of Kanaan Ministries South Africa, wrote about the necessity to renounce the 12 Zodiac signs. She shows how the four elements: Water, Wind, Earth and Fire are manipulated by the enemy in her book- The Four Elements. Numerous other writers such as John Eckhardt (Prayers That Rout Demons) Judson Cornwall (Worship as Jesus taught it) Dr, Myles Munroe (The Purpose and Power of Praise and Worship) and so many others all help us in our walk, worship and life in the Lord Jesus Christ. What makes them even more authentic is that they are thoroughly corroborated by Scriptures.

While this book gives the specific assignment of the principalities and powers in a general sense, it does not exhaust the full magnitude of their operations. JP Timmons, Amanda Buys, and Judson Cornwall works will be the main books quoted from and used in this book. It is by comparing these and other books/works with the bible that this book is constructed. However, always remember the focus of this book is about enhancing the believer's worship experience with the Lord Jesus Christ and being changed into His image. We must not become absorbed in satan's business as this is what he uses to distract from us from our purpose. We must press unto the prize of the high calling in Christ Jesus and desire His divine nature so much we no longer live---but Christ lives His life in us daily.

All believers have been given authority by Christ to address the spirit realm for He Jesus created it and all things. (Colossians 1:16) To challenge a believer on this matter whether young or old in the faith whether Apostle or just a church member is to challenge Jesus Christ Himself. He chose not many learned but the simple ordinary people of His day to train and take the gospel message. Many were fishermen such as Peter, James and John, traders of cloth example Lydia. Jesus warned them to beware of the yeast (teaching) of the learned religious people—the Scribes and the Pharisees. The Apostle Paul counted all his learning as but dung that he might gain Christ (he was the epitome of learning having studied under Gamaliel the chief intellectual of the Laws of God) Jesus told us to expect criticism and opposition as this is one of the surest sign that we are right on target. He Himself experienced the same when He was on Earth but He OVERCAME THEM ALL. Amen. All Christians can say without a doubt that at some point or the other they encountered demonic opposition and had to be prayed for and go through deliverance. No one is an 'expert' on this because God uses the foolish things to confound the wise and the weak things to overthrow the things that are mighty. However all are mandated by God to be equipped and not be ignorant of the enemy's devices.

To summarize all the foregoing theories and concepts presented here in this book I can say with absolute authority from the Word of God that they are true, believable and verifiable. This is because THIS IS NOT A RELIGIOUS BOOK even though it falls under the category of religion just for the sake of semantics Firstly, evil and demons exist since the fall of Lucifer. Though not seen physically they affect the lives of all mankind. Even non-christians have alluded to real encounters with wicked malevolent spirits especially those who were involved in witchcraft at any level of the occult. In the Book of Genesis 6: 1--8 it records that fallen angels came to earth, had sex with the daughters of men and produced a hybrid offspring of man and demonic---there were giants in the land and this is one reason God had to destroy the earth with the Flood in Noah's time. Jesus cast out a demonic group called Legion (about 6000 demons) from one man in a graveyard and many others during His daily ministry. The Apostle Paul rebuked and cast out a spirit of divination from the damsel in Ephesus. Even unto now in these modern days as people call it numerous cases of the weird, perverse and wicked acts of evil spirits can be read about on the internet, in thousands of books, and numerous cases of church leaders especially those in the deliverance ministries. They all testify and confirm what God's Word says. Jesus FINAL COMMISSION TO HIS CHURH INCLUDED----IN MY NAME CAST OUT DEVILS, HEAL THE SICK AND RAISE THE DEAD AND LO I AM WITH YOU ALWAYS EVEN UNTO THE END OF THE WORLD. Therefore let us be encouraged in the Lord always and do His Blessed Will until He returns.

CHAPTER ONE

What then is Worship?

Worship is to give the highest regard, reverence and obedience to Someone perceived to be the Greatest or Supreme Deity among mankind. It is done based on the belief that all life, power and blessings flow from this one Source or Creator to the creature. Various religions have contrived to promulgate a myriad of false, empty worship that does not satisfy the emptiness of the soul. Man was designed to worship Someone or Something. There is a God-shaped vacuum in man that only God can fill. We have heard this time and again but still words alone would fail to really describe what worship really is. This is because it is a constantly unfolding experience between the worshipper and the One being worshipped. All the books that man can write cannot plumb the depths of a true worship experience. Worship cannot be explained it can only be experienced. It is the most vital and precious possession of the worshipper. After a while it is impossible to separate the worshipper and the worshipped One. For the Body of Christ this is so aptly expressed in this scripture "For in Him we live and move and have our being" Acts 17:28 KJV—not just an occasional visit to the Holy of holies or the throne room of God.

Worship is not an emotion to be captured. We can't catch the spirit. It does involve our emotions as we are always affected by worship. Rather, He catches our spirits away into a glorious realm of release that is different from the previous worship experience. This is why we do not "camp out" and become stationary at the last time, spot or place of our last encounter. We cannot duplicate it. We have to flow with the Spirit of God---move with the Cloud and not with the Crowd. We do not compare or compete with one another when we worship God. We are too busy having a one and one experience of our very own with the Lord to really notice what's happening next to us. This is because we are not spectators but participants in worship.

Each worship experience is so precious and unique that we become highly excited and expectant for the next one. Babes drink at the breast of their mothers. So the worshippers drink at the fountain of the Many Breasted One. All our being is involved as we revel in the wonder and glory of being enveloped in His Presence as we prostrate in His Holy Presence. God does not need our worship to be God. He is the Self-existing, Self-sufficient One needing no one to make Him God. However we need to worship Him to show us who we are, why we exist and where we will eventually be in eternity. He is like the oxygen we breathe because we need oxygen to live. Without oxygen we die physically. Without worshipping Him we die spiritually. Whoever has the Son hath life, who doesn't have the Son the wrath of God abides in him (John 5:12) Worship then must be the lifestyle of the believer.

Worshipping God has nothing to do with being intellectually brilliant, fully learned in with man, it originated with God. God uses the worship He receives from man and does things with it for the good of mankind. When worshippers take their focus away from God and quench the Holy Spirit, it ceases to be a worship experience. The worshippers worship worship and praise praise and not the object of worship—Jesus Christ. They worship the praisers, dancers and instruments etc. This is always a sign of the presence of Lucifer in the service. Suddenly disagreements break out. There is rivalry and jealousy, bickering and faultfinding. People look around feeling bewildered. How did this happen? How can it be prevented from happening again? This and more along these lines is explained in later chapters especially chapter 6.

Worshipping God in a particular aspect of His nature and character gives us access for Him to meet that specific related need in our lives. Judson Cornwall points this out clearly in his book –"Worship as Jesus taught It". In chapter 10 he relates that when the Roman ruler came and worshipped Jesus in His revealed nature as the Source of life after his daughter had just died she was raised from the dead. Thus our need may be to be changed from a worried, anxious person to one who is reassured that things will work out well even if you don't know how, when or why. So you approach God with scriptures and songs that deal with this need. An example will suffice. You may need peace so you sing for example the song----

Jehovah Shamah you are my peace, Jehovah Shamah you are my Peace

For healing the song by Don Moen---I am the Lord that healeth thee, I am the lord

your healer I sent my word and healed your disease
I am the Lord your healer.

For victory in warfare----Hail, Hail Lion of Judah
how powerful you are.

However, worship must not be used as an excuse to use
God as we would use a credit card at a bank or store. We
must desire the Healer more than the healing, the Giver
more than the gift, the Blesser more than the blessing. We
must desire Him for who He is more than what he can do
for us. If you have children who only come to you when
they have a need, you feel they only want you for what you
can give them not for your intrinsic value. True worshippers
will seek to be in God's presence just for who He is---no one
else is like Him at all. His very presence enraptures them.

When you find yourself being excited about the next
worship experience and cannot wait for it to happen you know
that you are maturing. You are being built up of your own free
will and choice. No one is forcing you and you don't have to
work up your emotions. You don't care if it's snowing really
hard outside and the plumbing needs to be fixed. You are being
liberated from form, tradition, ritual, and worldly cares. Praise
the Lord. If only two persons are present or ten thousand it
doesn't matter. If it's in a basement or a five star hotel or a
place in the park it's a non issue. What causes the insatiable
hunger and thirst of worshippers is to be in God's present
presence----where He is what He is saying, doing and wants.
It's all about Him and not about us. Worship can be loud and
gloriously noisy, it can be quiet and reflective, it can be just
silence, dancing or whatever the Lord wills gets done. However
it's certainly not based on outward performance and especially
those that veer off into weird and questionable activities.

We can worship anywhere, anytime. Worship is not confined to the church building, or the cell group meeting. Worshipping God must come so natural to us that the place doesn't matter. Some Christians such as Ed Corley have learnt to think in tongues----swallow it down in the belly. This leaves mind free to concentrate on persons being prayed for and incredible discernment and revelation can be gained. We would be enthralled at what great things God can accomplish through us. Most of all the anointing rests on us continuously in worship and builds us up mightily. We are not laboring under the cares of this world. We are walking on water as Peter did. Think of all the many glorious opportunities we missed in our Christian walk because we did not know or understand the powerful connection we have with God when we worship Him. Our job environment would have been so different, our relationships would have been healed and improved and our dependence upon God most of all would have become absolutely critical and necessary to us.

We understand how powerful worship is when we study the life of David who wrote the Psalms. David built a tent in his backyard and appointed singers, dancers and praisers to worship God 24 hours a day, 7 days a week, 4 weeks a months, 12 months a year—all year round. This pleased the Lord so much that its one of the reasons God said David was a man after His own heart. David's many victories in battle were attributed to this permanent praise tent he set up. He lived under an open heaven. He was able to hear more clearly from God because the "high praises" of God was in his mouth and a two edged sword in his hand. He even said "let the saints sing aloud upon their beds (Psalm 149: 5 KJV). David danced before the Lord when the Ark of the Covenant returned to Israel (2 Samuel 6:14 KJV). It shows the value David placed on worshipping God continually. He was never weary or bored by it but experienced the highly coveted virtues and blessings from being a true worshipper of God.

Abraham is another example of what worship is and does for us. He was so transformed that he was willing to offer up his son Isaac as a sacrifice until God provided a ram instead. Moses worshipped God until his face shone so much they could not gaze at him. We have become too sufficient unto ourselves, our ministries, our callings, our jobs etc. We've built our little empires and expect God to signature it, just because His name is on the letterhead. We forget to worship Him for Whom He is. We cannot put God into our little boxes called our existence. We have to "leave it all behind" when it comes to our worship. If we truly want to be changed into His image then The Potter must be allowed to fashion the clay how He wants it. If we truly love Him and want Him we will allow Him to have His complete way in our daily lives.

When we worship God we receive divine and precise expressions of God's will via the revelations we experience. Jesus said ---- 'I do nothing of Myself except The Father first shows it to Me (John 5:19 KJV) Jesus spent quality time in the Father's presence as oftentimes He would go up into the mountains to pray especially at night. He got all His instructions from these divine encounters because in Him dwelleth "all the fullness of the Godhead bodily". Jesus often prayed when men were asleep, when the forces of darkness were raging. As the Son of man on earth He had to fulfill all requirements of prayer, fasting and seeking God as an example and pattern of what mankind should do. Therefore everything Jesus said and did proceeded directly from Father God on the throne in heaven. All the miracles

He did example healing the lame, deaf, dumb and raising the dead, He had the revelation beforehand that this is what God wanted done. Nothing happened by chance or accident but by divinely pre-determined design. This must be the daily experience of the believer on the individual and corporate level. To know we must worship and to worship we must make quality time for God seeking earnestly to know and do his blessed will daily.

J P Timmons in his book ----Mysterious Secrets of the Kingdom of Darkness chapter 7 and Amanda Buys in her book---The Four Elements state clearly that principalities and power[1]s meet daily planning and carrying out their assignment with terrible punishments when the demons fail. They speak out curses and [2]are highly organized in hierarchical structure. For example---Apollyon is in charge of all false religions and therefore collects all false worship from these heathen worshippers. He works with Ashtoreth/ Diana the same principality that the Apostle Paul confronted in Ephesus that was using the woman with the familiar spirit of divination. These principalities cover entire areas and attack the worship of the Body of Christ. They block the worship in the heavenlies using the forces of the 12 Zodiac signs and the Four Elements among other devices even when there is no sin in the lives of the Christians. This is because the heavenlies have been programmed. All mankind is born with natural bondages to the second heaven. They release curses, evil decrees and prophecies over the whole earth. They must be identified specifically by name and

---

[1]   JP Timmons, Mysterious Secrets of the Dark Kingdom: the battle for planet Earth(Manchaca: CCI Publishing 1991) pg 94

[2]   Amanda Buys, The Four Elements: (Capetown: Product of Kanaan Ministries, 2003) pg 39

assignment and be made divinely deaf, dumb and blind. All communication lines must be cut with the sword of the Spirit and the Blood of Jesus Christ. We can use this as an example and as the Lord leads (remember its always with the leading of the Lord).

> Father we come to you to wash and cleanse us of any sin we have committed and we renounce it in the Name and Blood Stripes of Jesus. In the Mighty Name of Jesus we take authority over Baal and Ashtoreth in the heavenlies. We bind your operations in this worship service of the true and only God—the Lord Jesus Christ. We render you deaf, dumb, blind and powerless in the Name and Blood of Jesus Christ. We break all your communication lines. Holy Spirit let your worship flow through us so that we will resist the devil, Baal and Ashtoreth and all other related powers"

This is why we cannot lead ourselves in worship. It is always the Spirit who prays and groans within us for He knoweth the Mind and will of God. However as stated before we must know their specific names, assignments and strongholds and must not be ignorant of the enemy's devices.

The worship of God by the Body of Christ must involve a strategic warfare knowledge based plan. Knowledge of the programming of the heavenlies is very important for serious contenders of biblical worship. Remember it was the issue of worship that led to the fall of Lucifer in the first place. It was not about what color God is, how many angels He has or of a particular angel example Michael or Gabriel. The whole fight began about who should receive worship. Remember Lucifer was able to influence 1/3 of the angels of God in this rebellion. He is called the god of this world because he receives worship from sinners of whom the majority of the inhabitants of the world are classified. This is either by a)willful choice (some cults teach Lucifer as god example Free masonry) b) ignorance(people see things as harmless example Ouija board, Harry Potter books astrology etc c) when people sin knowingly or unknowingly its giving the devil worship (1 John 3: 8 KJV)

This means everyone under the curse of the fallen nature who is not yet regenerated or born again is in this state. Lucifer programmed the heavenlies to suit his evil design after he was cast out of heaven. For ages of time, cycles of evil intent have been carried out almost uninterrupted and the church was not able to live under an open heaven as God designed. Those few interruptions included Elijah who was able to open and shut the heavens, Joshua who told the sun to stand still and it did, Deborah who commanded the stars to fight against Sisera. She faced down 900 chariots of iron (the stars strayed from their courses and the rivers washed Sisera's armies away in a massive flood).

The original scenario was that all creation was worshipping God in full magnitude and splendor---sun, moon, stars, wind, hail, fire, water, snow, hills trees planets, galaxies etc. The Psalmist declares—the heavens declare the glory of God –Psalm 19:1 KJV. There was such unparalleled harmony with God and nature that the morning stars sang together----Job 38:7 KJV---. All gave glory, honor and reverence to God Almighty alone-----2 Corinthians 1:4 KJV, Revelation 2:8 KJV. Lucifer coveted this worship because of jealousy and pride. This sin of pride entered mankind and led them away from the true Person and Object of worship-----God to the creature or created thing. The enemy has been perfecting this art of diverting worship. He makes people feel it has to follow a prescribed formula, or working up of the emotions. It is a deliberate choice we make with our wills that we worship the Lord exclusively. True worshippers discover such release in worshipping God He becomes their magnificent obsession.

The songwriter Helen Lemel says----'-Turn your eyes upon Jesus, and the things of this world will grow strangely dim, in the light of his glory and grace.' There is a shifting around of the circumstances we are currently in—they grow strangely dim. We feel as though a weight has been lifted and a fresh supply of God's Spirit comes to us. Then there is the awe of His presence----we just bask and wait there wanting to remain there and tarry. This tarrying is so crucial to what the Lord will reveal we must not make the mistake of running out of the presence of the Lord. The enemy likes to fool us that we have reached the ceiling or cutting off point of worship. However, this is just the first level. We must press in for more of Him. If we cannot, then sin and/or the enemy is the cause. In the Holy of Holies we do nothing, say nothing, we just receive God's will for that particular worship experience.

Paul and Silas worship experience alluded to earlier was produced under severe hardship and cruelty. They were beaten and put in prison for preaching the Gospel. But they were counting it all joy to be persecuted for Christ's sake. When the prisoners remained even after the earthquake shook the doors open it was because of the worship. We never know where our worship experience will take us so it's always something to look forward to. The flesh is always warring against the spirit. People keep looking at their clocks during a worship service. They focus on the lunch simmering in the oven or the children to get ready for school. They rush off after the service. They work late at the office Monday nights and some still get laid off the job. Now when they face this persecution of unemployment they can't praise God like Paul and Silas did. They now want the whole church to pray and tarry in God's presence to get 'a word from the Lord. We are all guilty of this wayward wandering in the wilderness of the flesh. We have to kill these giants in our flesh to enter the Promised Land of the Holy Spirit. The flesh bawls in the Outer Court as it is put to death but our spirit cries out to God for fulfillment.

The enemy brings his assaults on our desires and appetites and every undisciplined area of our being. The Apostle Paul had a simple solution. He said—"-I die daily that Christ may live in me "(1 Corinthians 15:31KJV). He also shows how effective speaking in tongues is more than his natural language. Note that he did this daily while for many of us it's only a day or two before Sunday as we prepare for the Lord's Day worship service. While home, family work and career are vital concerns for us we are far too busy and burnt out with worldly cares to be effective worshippers. We must be yoked to the Lord in such a way that we actually enter into His Rest. Then we really worship and cease from our labors (Hebrews 4: 11 KJV). In other words God has our entire lives mapped out in this way. It is a finished product which we simply receive by faith and thanksgiving. We can live carefree lives now albeit not careless lives.

This worship experience daily enables us to dwell with God continuously as we are seated with Christ in heavenly places. We have to utilize this gift of privilege to reign over principalities and powers in the heavenly places. It enables us to decree, legislate and exercise jurisdictional authority in Christ Name and Power. The realm of Politics, Finance, Law Education, Music Sports, Family Life, Trade, Industry, Science/Technology, Military, Travel, Health etc have all been hijacked/influenced by the kingdom of Darkness. Satan and his principalities and powers uses these structures to govern the affairs of mankind still believing he is god. Sin of course gives him this right. But once the Gospel of the Kingdom of God reaches and changes every heart then the kingdoms of this world have now become the kingdom of our God and of His Christ (Revelation 11;15. KJV)

Christ worshippers will bind their kings and nobles with fetters of iron (Psalm 149:8 KJV) as the high praises of God ascend to His throne.

CHAPTER TWO

Heaven's Original Worship Experience

The Bible describes the Creation Story in the first book –Genesis- from which we first glimpse the original created order and the beauty of it all is based on the worship of God the Creator.

We see that from nothing and chaos (Genesis 1:2 KJV) God filled the empty sky with the sun, moon, stars, rain, snow thunder, lightning, planets and galaxies. They are all regulated by the four seasons—Spring, Summer, Autumn and Winter. We see Him fill the earth with vegetation and trees, herbs, flowers, oceans, rivers, mountains, hills and all the beasts of the field. It was a marvelous masterpiece. The creature gave the Creator worship (Psalm 19: 12) the heavens declare the glory of God and the firmament shows His handiwork. The morning stars sang together. There was constant worship before God's throne day and night even as it is unto now and ever shall be. God uses this worship to keep the universe in order and stability. Out of this worship comes His Word revealed because worship reveals Him and

His will and the angels hearken unto His voice and carries out His Word (Psalm 103: 20 KJV).

God is Self-Existing and the Self-Sufficient One. He doesn't need the worship of men to make Him God but the created man, creature or thing needs to worship Him in order to exist.(Psalm 150: 6 KJV) states-----"Let everything that hath breath praise the Lord". Thus when the angels and the elders sing—"You are worthy to receive Glory, honor and power" their praise becomes His Word in all the earth and His Word becomes Law,---fixed, final. We see Jesus, this Word which was from the beginning, being made flesh. He came to the earth and redeemed all mankind and is therefore having all these qualities and is worthy of the worship He receives. Heaven and earth shall pass away but not one tit or part of His Word shall pass away. God is eternal and His worship never ceases.

CHAPTER THREE

What caused Lucifer to Fall?

Pride versus Humility

Pride is listed among the seven things which God hates as stated in Proverbs 6: 16—19 KJV. This sin is so great in the eyes of God that God cast Lucifer out of heaven via the Archangel Michael. Pride has a way of totally blinding an individual that they do not see their fall coming (Proverbs 16:18 KJV) pride goeth before a fall and a haughty spirit before destruction. Most mental and emotional problems people experience have their root cause in pride and self-centeredness. Mankind with the fallen Adamic nature pursues the path of life led mainly by his five senses and the pride oriented ego. Then comes the baggage of performance oriented living to be accepted by others. How easily the emotions are hurt and vulnerable because of pride being the cause. We have to learn to differentiate. We have to learn to love ourselves by accepting our value from the Cross.

Lucifer always appeal to the pride in man's soul to make him think he can live independent of God and make it through life on his own merit and accomplishments. The relentless cycle of compare and compete to be better than the rest takes man on a path of constant striving without being fulfilled. Lucifer's pride was based on his wisdom and beauty given to him by God. Had he continued to use it for God he would still be in heaven worshipping God with the other angels As long as we are focused on God our attention is drawn away from self and to God our creator. We worship Him simply for who He is and what He stands for and wants done---service to others. An example will suffice here. It is impossible to be in God's presence worshipping Him and then come out for example, and drive our car recklessly and kill or injure a person. Rather we would come out and pick up an injured person who was hit by someone else and we take them to the hospital. We make the extra time for them because worship helps Christ to live His life through us. We are not focused on how expensive our car may be to put a virtual stranger in who may not look or smell good.

The pride that Lucifer had was dangerous in that he rebelled against God becoming accusatory, arrogant and murderous. Jealousy arose in him. He convinced 1/3 of the angels to follow him in his rebellion. The desire to be in control of everything at any cost, sparing no one but concealing all this with deception and lies as an angel of light made witchcraft second nature to Lucifer. Rebellion is as the sin of witchcraft (1 Samuel 15: 23. KJV) Then to impart this nature to man (to be independent and to control others, being your own god) via the Garden of Eden experience, became Lucifer's obsession. He beguiled Eve. He went to her in the form of a serpent.

Leviathan is referred to in the Bible as the chief Spirit of pride-- Satan in the form of a serpent. Leviathan tempted Eve until she ate of the tree of the knowledge of Good and Evil and gave to Adam her husband. Their eyes were 'opened' to the pride of knowing something they felt should have been given to them by God from the beginning. Instead of humbling themselves with the comforting reality that their All Wise All Loving Creator must have a very good reason for forbidding them to eat from the tree. Their hearts were filled with pride. I am my own god, I don't need God. The god of this world blinded them to their impending fall and banishment from the Garden of Eden. Isn't it revealing that pride puts distance and alienation between God and man more than any other sin? Psalm 138: 6 KJV says God sees them from afar off.

Therefore, one of the first requirements of man in his yearning to be re-united with God is to love mercy and truth and to walk humbly with thy God (Micah 6: 8. KJV) A proud arrogant person is always imposing their will on others. They always have to look good at somebody's expense. To preserve their image and status quo they always revert to their pride. Next comes the bondage of who is superior to whom. Men are put in dictatorial positions over others to maintain the 'balance of pride". People's values do become so subtly rooted in pride that a good thing becomes motivated by a bad thing. For example, people value education but pride of knowledge prevents them from using that knowledge to truly help others. They fear that they would be replaced. There should be no fear of replacement in the first place. The trick that Lucifer plays on mankind is to make humility look weak, stupid, demeaning, dehumanizing and devaluing. However, this is really what pride is. People naturally cringe in revulsion and fear when they are told to humble themselves and speak the truth especially when it's embarrassing. Fear is now linked to humility when it should be pride.

Man's psyche now was polluted with pride, rebellion and fear. Lucifer's stronghold in the mind was cunningly construed. It became easy to play the blame game even now. Pride keeps self on the throne and Jesus on the Cross when it should be vice versa. Pride causes people to refuse to forgive even though God has commanded it and will help us through the process as we in our own strength cannot do it. Forgiveness did not originate with man but with God who knew from the beginning that man would need this virtue.

With pride so well entrenched in the human system, each man became a law unto himself. God's laws are ignored and lawlessness results. Pride is the root cause of all rebellion. To continue in rebellion mankind would use any means at his disposal to maintain it. This is why witchcraft is so appealing to the cursed Adamic nature. It enables man to manipulate man and circumstances to be in control or to be controlling. We wonder why people are so prone to be involved in witchcraft, but this should be no wonder. The scriptures lists witchcraft as one of the natural works of the flesh (Galatians 5:20KJV). Witchcraft is so natural to human nature, it disguises itself as part of the human charisma and is never properly challenged.

The scriptures exhort the believers to overcome the lust of the eye, the lust of the flesh and the pride of life (1 John 2: 16. KJV) Even the normal everyday conversation of people have self at the center so often. Typical statements such as— "Look what I have achieved, I have a PHD from Harvard University. I just bought my new car etc demonstrate this fact. Rather they should be re-phrased with—As By the grace of God I have a PHD from Harvard University or with the help of my parents I've bought my new car.

Even humility can be controlled by pride in the carnal nature of mankind. People can boast about how humble they are while all the time not realizing that pride is at the root of their confessions. They boast about all the poor they have fed, the homeless they have sheltered and so on. Like the publican in the Bible, self-centeredness of human nature is on display and will not be easily silenced. The scriptures warn us (do not do your alms before men (Matthew 6: 1 KJV) and do not let your right hand know what your left hand is doing (Matthew 6:3. KJV)

Lucifer came to Eve in the form of a snake. She was beguiled and deceived. Snakes are naturally revolting. People kill them instantly. If a snake gets away and is lurking somewhere nearby people feel uneasy until it is searched out and destroyed. But people go to bed with pride in their hearts, wake up with it next morning and go through the day with it quite comfortably. John the Baptist called his generation a generation of vipers. This demonstrates how seriously and vividly how we in the Body of Christ must deal with pride. We must kill it by crucifying the flesh just as we would kill a natural snake. The word lust appears twice in one scripture (1 John 2:16 KJV—the lust of the eye, the lust of the flesh and the pride of life). Lust denotes a strong desire and drive to have something that is not really good for us. It embraces the sensual which borders unto what is base and untrustworthy. This is what was imparted in the Garden---to live by pride and the five senses (humanism)] rather than by the divine nature and revelation and obedience to God.

Behold, I give unto you power to trample on snakes and scorpions and over all the power of the enemy and nothing shall by any means harm you. (Luke 10:19. KJV) You will trample on the lion and the adder the young lion and the dragon you will trample underfoot (Psalms 91:13KJV). This gives us marvelous insight into how to trample the enemy of our souls who fell because of pride. The serpent in the Garden becomes the dragon in Revelation 20:2. We are commanded to trample on the snake, lion and dragon.

Trample means to pound into a pulp, to thresh out, flatten out and tread firmly upon. You cannot be under it but over it from above. If you are not above you have to jump high enough for trample means to descend upon something from a higher point.

The Body of Christ must trample on the dragon (satan) with many heads in the book of Revelation 12:3-5 KJV who goes after the woman with child [the Church]. He spews out a flood to swallow her up but she is caught up to the throne of God for in her is the Man-child (Jesus) fully formed in her. The Church is fully transformed into His image. Jesus the Seed of the woman came and bruised his head—government. Jesus the Man-child in His Church is putting the final touches to the bruising of the Dragon's head before His return giving us a foretaste as it were of what it feels like to wield power over satan and his principalities and powers.

To really enter into this fullness of trampling the Dragon the Body of Christ must deal with sin especially the sin of pride more seriously than ever.

CHAPTER FOUR

And there was War in Heaven

Interestingly enough the first war to ever occur in the universe was due to pride. Lucifer's pride led him in his rebellion with 1/3 of the angels to take the throne of God. Imagine he made five attempts to do so as recorded in the Book of Isaiah 14: 12—17 KJV.

To be God means that all creation must worship Him and therefore God reigns, rules and governs based on loving, willing and obedient worship given to Him. Amen. War is a state of conflict, battle, and contention between two or more opposing forces. Everyone wants to know why they are at war—the cause, the reason. Desire for power is not bad but it is the motivation behind it that is pivotal. The drive for power to replace God is ludicrous because the creature is not greater than the Creator neither can he replace Him. For 1/3 of the angels to be deceived by Lucifer shows the great wisdom and influence he had but we must always remember he got it from God. Therefore, God who is without beginning or end is greater by far for God cannot be measured.

The battle for the throne of God was serious, intensely catastrophic. The earth had to be re-created (Genesis 1: 1–2. KJV) The Book of Job clearly shows it led to the devastation of the earth, mountains, waters etc. The earth was now without form and void and darkness was on the face of the deep. The five I wills of the devil reads thus from Isaiah 14:13-14 KJV---For thou has said in thine heart, I will ascend to heaven, I will exalt my throne above the stars of God, I will sit upon the mount of the congregation in the sides of the north, I will ascend above the heights of the clouds, I will be like the Most High. The words ascend, exalt, sit upon the mount, ascend and will be like the Most High reveals the first great flaw of Lucifer's plan to become God. God did not have to do something to become God. He did not have to ascend, exalt, or sit or do anything to be God. He is God (State Of Being) Without Beginning or End, father or mother. Mary was the mother of Jesus the Son in the physical body but she was not the mother of God. So God had to make over a new earth.

When he was cast down to earth the Bible predicts woe to the inhabitants of the earth for the devil has come down with great wrath (Revelation 12: 12). War was instituted on earth via the Luciferian governments of the earth—Free Masonry, the Illuminati and Secret Societies. Every nation feels threatened by another and build huge weaponry bases to defend itself in the event of an attack on its sovereignity. These societies fund all the wars and exercise secret control thereby. The whole structure of society, Health, Education, Law Trade, Politics etc are secretly manipulated by the satanic government. However God is still on the throne and Jesus Christ is Head of all Principality and Power having complete and sovereign rule over all things in heaven and earth having all enemies under His feet. Jesus promises 'I will build My Church and the gates of hell shall not prevail against it (Matthew 11:18 KJV). The earth is His footstool and through His Church God will make known His will----that unto the principalities and powers might be made known the manifold wisdom of God (Ephesians 3: 10 KJV)

Jesus victory over principalities and powers is complete. They have been thoroughly wounded and stripped of their power, rule and authority by the legality of the will which is in the BLOOD OF THE TESTATOR---JESUS CHRIST THE RIGHTEOUS. This was completed by Christ Jesus and the finished work of the Cross. Wherefore God hath highly exalted Him and given Him a name that at the Name of Jesus every knee should bow and every tongue confess that Jesus Christ is Lord to the glory of God the Father. This they know and accept as uncontestable. They must fight against the church and the spreading of the Gospel to maintain major control over the governments of the world.

They work to make the church look weak, irrelevant, archaic and even-nonexistent claiming all church related issues ended with the death of the Apostles. The Book of Revelation was particularly targeted by the Dark Kingdom as it shows so graphically the Lord Jesus Christ as King of Kings and Lord of Lords through all past and present kingdoms with His Kingdom on earth to put a final end to all kingdoms. Therefore the war in the second heaven moves to the war on earth.

The war is heavily spiritual even though the physical man-made weapons are state of the art scientific breakthroughs. But the same God who delivered the children of Israel across the Red Sea with only the lifted rod of His servant Moses was able to drown horse and chariot of Pharaoh's army. And most importantly God is always full of surprises and awesome miracles working in ways far beyond the comprehension of man or satan. As the Body of Christ bear His image in the earth and do His works exercising our Blood bought rights we appreciate more fully the necessity of our worship connection to Christ. We can and will do exploits through Him who enables us. God uses the foolish things to confound the wise and the weak things to overthrow the mighty.

Can you imagine winning a battle with a loaf of barley? (Judges 7:13, KJV) bringing down a giant with a sling as David did to Goliath? Can satellites, computers, rockets, missiles digitalizing of society, chemical and nuclear weapons intimidate God? Certainly not! Where is the disputer of this world, God is confounds the wisdom of the wise and brings to naught the understanding of the prudent. He turns all to foolishness. (1 Corinthians 1: 27 KJV)

Chapter Five

What did Lucifer do after His Fall?

Having been cast out of heaven, Lucifer set out to build his kingdom in the heavenlies---the Second Heaven, while he roams up and down the earth seeking whom he may devour (1Peter 5:8. KJV) As the Body of Christ we must know our assignment. Lucifer set up a kingdom in total rebellion against God's created order. We must have knowledge of which principality and power is in charge of what.

Lucifer's nature was totally opposite to the divine nature. It was evil and corrupt full of lies blasphemy and accusations. He was perfect until iniquity was found in him. He was a murderer from the beginning and he abode not in the truth. The double nature of light and darkness, the idea that there is no evil, it depends on the circumstances came from him. It is a departure from the moral absolutes of God and His divine nature. By listening to and agreeing with him man falls into the default mode because the mind becomes blinded to truth and God's standard of reality.

So what did he do after the fall? He continued to believe he is God and continued to influence 1/3 of the angels to rebel against God. Darkness entered the universe. Negative and evil thoughts permeated the second heaven. Violence and malevolence and wickedness crouched in every corner waiting to be expressed on the earth. Lucifer became the Father of lies and comes to kill steal and destroy. The world became a wilderness, a devastated and barren place. The very creation began to rebel against nature and their Creator. Even as Jesus is the fullness of the Godhead bodily so Lucifer is the fullness of iniquity and evil bodily reaching its height in the anti-christ.

The satanic government hijacked the sun, moon, stars, and planets and seasons to program the heavenlies in a counter- productive manner and to rebel against God's design. Sin and death was programmed into the heavenlies because he sinneth from the beginning. By being a bully and a terror (a roaring lion) or a deceptive liar (angel of light) he thus controlled the cosmos—he became the god of this world. Always remember the devil copies God's original plan as much as he can and uses disguise to mask the real evil intent. God made the heavens and the earth before He created man. Satan programmed the planetary system to serve his evil intent to snare mankind. He used the wisdom God gave him to do this and God in His sovereignity allowed him. All this was embodied in the tree of the Knowledge of Good and Evil which God forbid them to eat of for in the day they did they would die.

God—The Lord Jesus Christ is so all wise (Omniscient) He can use Lucifer's wisdom against him. He turns it to foolishness as He wills and sends diviners mad. He allowed Lucifer to go ahead with his plan to be the god of this world and gave mankind a will to choose who he would follow.

God knows His creation best. He knows that mankind does not like pain, suffering, sickness, poverty, shame, death and all the woes that would result from mankind listening to the enemy in the Garden. God knows His creation would love life, health, glory etc and would choose this in Christ Jesus when He would come to earth and give His Life as the Perfect Sacrifice. This would foil the plan of the enemy finally and totally. This is why Lucifer had to beguile Eve about his real intention.

God knew that Lucifer would use the sun, moon, stars etc to set up the zodiac signs and thereby cause a natural bondage in mankind no matter what time [month of the year] they were born into because already man was born and shapen in iniquity. This manipulation would extend to the four major elements—water, earth, fire and wind. When God planted the tree of the knowledge of Good and Evil in the Garden He knew that when they ate of it (partaking of forbidden knowledge of the occult, false religion), this would give satan the legal right to activate the constellations, the zodiac signs, the elements etc to co-operate with evil. All this was held in abeyance until they ate of the tree. The curse was programmed into the universe and began to rule over the destiny of the human race.

Many people (even in the Body of Christ) still do not fully understand how much sway these constellations have on entire nations. People shrug off and say----Oh I don't read my horoscope, I don't believe in that. That's fine but it's not the end of the matter. Your entire nation is controlled by different zodiac signs in the course of the year. That's why your nation has the kinds of problems it has. You go to church, read your Bible and pray for your nation but with little or no lasting change. You migrate to another country but experience similar or worse problems there.

Lucifer programmed the universe along occultic sorceries, witchcraft and magic. It's all inclusive, all pervasive right down to the clothes people wear, the food they eat etc. They wear designer clothes and have state of the art equipment and furniture that were designed with some element of evil in it----some of its manufacturers are Satanists. Even some of the medications we use today have serious side effects because of these curses. Harry Potter books are definitely hypnotic mind control in design and mislead children into fourth density occultic programming of their subconscious minds. Most of the toys and computer games are no different. The education system teaches that man came from apes through evolution. John Dewey, Sigmund Freud and several other psychologists were Free Masons who perpetrated in their theories in a very subtle way the lie of the god of self. For example Dewey showed that in a Child-centered education religion (God) must be left out. It's all a mixture in the sea of Humanism that man in his fallen state calls wisdom, enlightenment and progress.

Out of all these mixtures in the foundation of the educational philosophy come other modern day theories all based on do it for yourself realism, develop your potential independently without being accountable to anyone. You must find the you in you, have alternative lifestyles, it's okay to follow your desires even if and when they inflict harm and tragedy to others. Pro-abortionists, Feminism, Lesbianism, and Gay rights philosophies put pressure on Governments to pass laws granting same sex marriages in some states in America such as Idaho, Connecticut, Iowa, California and several others. All of this has one name –Humanism or in plain language –you are your own god, look to the godhood path of life and reincarnate if you want to.

Before all these things manifested in the physical realm they all existed in the spiritual and cosmic realm. To access it man has to consult with the "experts"—the astrologers, Free Masons, illuminati, worldly wise:---those who worship the sun, moon, stars etc—the creature rather than the Creator (Romans 1: 25).

When you think of which school, college or university you want to send your child to you find the same pervasive lies and deception being peddled in these systems which are highly influenced by the Illuminati. Slowly lies are replacing truth and values are twisted. People call right wrong and wrong right. The scripture warns against this in Isaiah 5:20 KJV. Our task as believers and members of the Body of Christ is to overthrow these systems with the truth which is the Word of God the Word of Life. And we do this as the Corporate Body of Christ that identifies which zodiac sign is controlling our nation (our political, religious and economic leaders) and bind their operations in our nation. Blessed is the nation whose God is the Lord (Psalm 33: 12—22 KJV) Blessed is the nation who has dismantled the programming over their land by taking the Blood of Jesus and blotting out the handwriting of ordinances that is against it. Now you can appreciate the need to see the study of the zodiac signs not just as a casual harmless activity that whacky people get involved in but as a deliberate malevolent design against your very existence on earth.

CHAPTER SIX

The Kingdom Government of Lucifer/Satan

All governmental authorities have some type of order or structure. There is the Head or Leader and those with delegated authority to carry out the wishes, rules and commands of the leader. The idea of hierarchy is not new and is entrenched in the philosophy of government The whole structure operates on the procedure of following the "chain of command" to carry out the functions of government. God's throne follows this order as the originator of all things including government. There is God on the throne with Archangels just beneath Him as the following diagram depicts and even the principalities and powers are beneath God but they operate in rebellion.

GOD ON THE THRONE

ARCHANGELS

MICHAEL   GABRIEL

CHERUBIM AND SERAPHIM

THRONES   THRONES   THRONES
THRONES   THRONES

PRINCIPALITIES AND POWERS

RULERS OF DARKNESS

SPIRITUAL HOSTS OF WICKEDNESS
IN HEAVENLY PLACES

God uses the operations of the principalities and powers against themselves. Whatever they do is no surprise to God, He knows the end from the beginning. He is able to use whatever they do to carry out His predetermined will. This is what makes Him God. Hallelujah! This is what makes God to win no matter which way things go. Lucifer knows he is going to the lake of fire with his fallen angels and demons and he has no power to stop or reverse it. Yet he is mad enough to say he is still God. He also uses this knowledge of his certain doom to take mankind along with him.

The Bible mentions these principalities and powers specifically and what they were involved in at the time these incidents were written as shown below. All scriptures listed below are from the King James Version (Authorized Version) KJV

Appollyon--------Job 26:16, 28: 22, 31:12, Psalm 88: 11, Proverbs15:11,Revelation 9:11
> Example Revelation 9:11 (he is the angel of the bottomless pit)

Abaddon-------- Proverbs 27:20 Revelation 9:11
> Example Proverbs 27:20 (hell and destruction are never full)

Leviathan------- Job 9:9, 38:31, 41, Psalm 74:14, Revelation 12:1-17, Genesis 1:20-23, Isaiah 27:1 (the Lord shall punish Leviathan with His great and strong sword)

The Beast------------ Revelation 13: 17,18, Rev 14: 9-11, Rev 20:4
> Example Revelation 13:17,18 (that no man can buy or sell unless he took Mark of the Beast which is triple six---666)

Beelzebub-------Mark 3:20—24, Matthew 12:22—24, Luke 11; 15
> Example Mark 3 20-24 (the scribes accuse Jesus of casting out demons by Beelzebub the prince of demons)

Jezebel---------2 Kings 9;22, 2 Kings 9: 30-37. 2 Kings 19:1-21, 25 Revelation 2:20
> Example Revelation 2:20 Jesus reproves the Church at Thyatira for having Jezebel in their midst who calls herself a prohetess to teach and seduce His servants to commit fornication and to eat things sacrificed unto idols

Gog and Magog------Ezekiel 38 Ezekiel 39
> Example Ezekiel 38 God says He is against Magog and will put hooks into his Jaws, and bring him forth with all his armies and in chapter 39 God says He is Against Gog and will turn him back and leave a sixth part of him.

Mammon------Matthew 6:24, Luke 16:9, 13
> Example Luke 16: 13 Jesus says no one can serve two masters—God and mammon

Ashtoreth-------------Revelation 11: 15, Jeremiah 7:18, Jeremiah 44: 17, 19, 25
> Example Jeremiah 7:18 (the children gather wood and the fathers kindle the Fire and the women knead dough to offer to the queen of heaven)

Baal-------------Judges 2:11, 10:10, 1Kings 18:18, Jeremiah 19:5, Hosea 2:17
> Example Jeremiah 19;5[they have built also the high places of Baal to burn their Sons with fire for burnt offerings unto Baal which I commanded not, nor spake it neither came it into my mind.

Molech-------1 Kings 11:7, Leviticus 20;2
> Example 1 Kings 11; 7 (Solomon built a high place for Molech the Abomination of the children of Ammon.)

Dagon---------1 Samuel 5;2
> Example 1 Samuel 5:2 (when the Philistines took the Ark of God, They brought it into the house of Dagon and set it by Dagon)

Belial-----------Judges 19:22,Judges 20: 13, 2 Corinth 6:15, Deut 13:13, 1 Sam 1:16,

The others listed below although they are not named specifically in the Bible fall under the general category of the many devils and demons mentioned. For example the Apostle Paul met a damsel with a familiar spirit at Ephesus which he discerned and immediately cast out.(the demon Paimon) Simon the sorcerer was struck with blindness (wizard) The lame man at the Gate(the demon Djoka) The 7 unclean spirits that Jesus [3]cast out of Mary Magdeline and the numerous examples of demonic confrontation the Apostles had with devils and demons and which present day ministers of God are still dealing with. These are the demonic spirits mentioned in JP Timmons Book- Mysterious Secrets of the Dark Kingdom.

a) Paimon-
b) Ashmodee
c) Ariton
d) Orionta
e) Ogeaso
f) Djoka
g) Tinka-
h) Arcarine
i) Queen Of The Coast-
j) Cyriel
k) Spirits of Islam

---

[3] JP Timmons, Mysterious Secrets of the dark kingdom. (Manchaca: CCI Publishing 1991) pgs 129--132

It should also be remembered that these spirits may have different names in different cultures and societies but they can still be identified once their assignment, activities and roles are observed. Then their names can be identified and they still can and must be cast out. One of the protocols of deliverance is that once there is legal grounds for the spirit to remain then it cannot be cast out. It must be renounced by those who are bound then and only then it will leave. Many people even christians are afraid to be embarrassed to reveal their involvement with the occult and prefer a game of hide and seek hoping for the best. However, there is no peaceful co-existence with the Kingdom of God and Light and the kingdom of darkness. There is always a all or none, do or die approach as the two are violently opposed to each other. Demons cannot stand worship, they will manifest or hinder the worship service to remain in hiding in the person or persons. This is why worship is such a battle for we are wrestling against those spirits who once worshipped God in heaven before they fell in rebellion with Lucifer. They hate worship with a passion.

CHAPTER SEVEN

The Deception of Adam and Eve and The Man Made Church

Adam and Eve we know enjoyed perfect fellowship with God in the Garden of Eden before they fell. The idea of being their own god lured them away from God into sin and death for their object and focus of worship was replaced by the god of self. All religion that developed after the fall of man pursued a humanistic and independent path to life to accomplish what they perceived to be the true purpose of life. Humanism and education replaced revelation knowledge that can only come from worshipping God in Spirit and in Truth. Other works of the flesh replaced the Spirit such as variance, witchcraft, seditions, emulations, heresies etc. When you remove truth all you have left is a lie. We know all lies come from the Father of lies. Man was led into religion and religiosity---this is his search for God and it is based on self effort, works of one's own righteousness and piety. All this we know from scripture is a total waste of time as all our righteousness is as filthy rags in His sight. (Isaiah 64:16 KJV)

Many theologians such as Watchman Nee discuss the latent power of the soul and show the close resemblance of soulish characteristics with spiritual attributes of the Lord Jesus Christ. Nee notes the example of the soul ruling the spiritual life via the five senses, man's talents and abilities without any intervention of the Holy Spirit whatsoever. The example of two servants of the Lord appointed to complete a task at church and which one depends on God the most as being spirit led is quite revealing. Servant A for example is a trained bookkeeper via education while Servant B knows very little about bookkeeping. Both are born again and Spirit filled. The Church selects Servant A of course to be the bookkeeper as he has the natural ability. However, he may not and often does not depend on the Holy Spirit for guidance. He already knows how to keep the books using his own ability. If Servant B is asked to do it in the absence of a Servant A type of person, will most certainly depend on the Holy spirit for guidance and is more likely to be in tune with the Lord's will for the task.

Mankind will keep using his natural talents and abilities in this fallen world until he reaches the end of his human resources and recognizes his need for divine help. The myriad of false gods and religions plunges him into deeper despair as he searches for God. The environment rules man because of the fall when he lost his dominion and authority. Jesus came to restore this authority. He did not come with another religion. e came to mend the breach by reconnecting man's worship experience with his Creator. Jesus knew the deception Lucifer caused in the soul realm of man---to depend on the latent power of the soul for his survival.

In the Garden of Eden man was deceived into using his reason, senses, emotions and will to meet life's needs without depending on God. In the man-made church today this is the number one problem---humanism. People depend on the soulish memories stored in the mind of previous times without any fresh impartation. They think they have reached the zenith of service when they follow a program written in textual form from the Bible usually in a hurry two or three days before the service date. Rote and routine becomes the order of the day as the principalities and powers such as Ashtaroth, Paimon, Apollyon and their subservient demons work to keep the service in the realm of humanism. Worship resists the devil and his hosts and allows the congregation to move into the place God wants them to be at that particular time and season.

Even after a church service has ended the Holy Spirit must be consulted to keep the unsurrendered soul from returning to its latent power base. The soul that is yoked to Christ and Christ alone is constantly enjoying the privileges of worship and it becomes difficult for principalities and powers to work because we can say like Jesus---"the evil one cometh and findeth nothing in Me (that he could pull on ---John 14: 30). The Word of God is quick and sharper than a two edged sword piercing asunder between spirit, soul and body. Liberty Savard's CDS and DVDS on---Binding and Loosing—has quite a unique insight in dealing with the unsurrendered soul. She speaks about binding ones will to the will of God, mind to the mind of Christ and emotions to the healing balance and overcoming behaviors of the Fruit of the Holy Spirit. This truly helps to cut asunder between spirit, soul and body.

Another deception to guard against in the man-made humanistic church is the illumination or false Luciferian light of those with Third Eye religious bondages. They imitate the true Apostolic gifts with false visions and words of knowledge. They use the information of familiar spirits which use zodiac/psychic readings, leylines etc to tell you your name, where you live and work, how much money you have in your pocket etc. Sometimes the counterfeit comes so close that if it were possible even the very elect would be deceived. This is why church services must have the following things done long before and just prior to its beginning according to Amanda Buys et al.

a) Silencing the 12 zodiac signs, asking God to send divine deafness, dumbness and blindness to them. Blot out all programming in the sun, moon, stars, pathways, orbits and their corridors of influence and power.

b) Cut their leylines and pulleys

c) Commanding that the latent power of the soul does not surface in the service but rather that wills, minds and emotions be bound to the will of God and mind of Christ

d) That before the service people share what God has laid on their hearts (the Outer court) because when we go to worship it is to worship Him for who He is and know His heart and will and mind exclusively, exclusively, exclusively. Amen.

CHAPTER EIGHT

The Worship Led Life is The Purpose Led Life

As alluded to earlier, everything we see is a product of worship. It depends on Who or what is being worshipped. God's people worship Him and adore him continuously and our lives become a reflection of that worship. We are able to demonstrate the Fruit of the Holy Spirit---Love, Joy, Peace, Temperance etc (Galatians 5: 22 KJV) even when things are not going the way we expect or want. That's when our lives become independent of our circumstances. Our worship of Jesus actually helps us to soar above these and still pursue our purpose. This is why the worship led life is the purpose driven life.

Those who worship in the Kingdom of Darkness worship the prince of darkness and his fallen angels. They too become a product of that negative energy. They demonstrate murder, violence, war, death, lawlessness etc. However they are not free because they can be bound in the Mighty Name of Jesus Christ. They are subject to a higher to a higher power of which they cannot escape. This is a major difference between the Kingdom of Darkness and the Kingdom of Light. They do not and cannot share equality as some proponents of duality advocate. Our superior worship of the Most High is so all powerful and boundless we can ascend in worship and descend in warfare over the Kingdom of Darkness at will as the Lord leads. We are always victorious through Christ Jesus. Praise the Lord.

When we study the lives of the Apostles we recognize that they were always led by the Holy Spirit to accomplish the things they did. The more they spent time in the Word with worshipful meditation the more they were imbued with power from on high. The Spirit always testified of Jesus—The Word. This gave them specific guidance as to the will of God for their lives at any particular time. Jesus said –"Without Me ye can do nothing (John 15:5 KJV). Therefore as we invite Him into our situations, decisions etc we find that as soon as we are connected to Him we begin to worship Him of our own accord. We can't but help it. We are engulfed in His presence. There is a difference in the atmosphere. We feel His Presence. We just want to let go and let Him have His way. It's the unforced rhythms of life that makes worshipping the Lord Jesus so easy and fulfilling. There is no struggle and no desire to entertain or to be facetious. We just flow with Him. We just flow with Him.

As we observe a river flowing we see it takes everything in its path in exactly the same direction it is going. Everything just gets carried along on a free transport ride as it were. The scripture alludes to the Holy Spirit as a river welling up within our innermost being. It has nothing to do with our moods, fancies, intellect or imagination. We can begin to speak in unknown tongues which praise the Lord does not originate with us either. Now the Holy Spirit speaks through us with groaning that cannot be uttered. Someone may begin to speak aloud above everyone else. There is a pause. Another will begin to interpret and reveal the mind of the Lord. We are all built up and edified and we are give fresh direction in our walk with the Lord.

Worship leads us in the perfect will of God. It's God's perfect safeguard for our own well being, growth and development. It's not the latent power of our souls. Neither is it our unsurrendered and naturally rebellious nature. We like our own way because we are self-willed by nature. Binding our wills to the will of God speaks of us no longer wanting to function in our own wills as it connotes the idea of being firmly fastened on to something as a nut and bolt are riveted together. We allow Christ to mind-control us willingly as it were. However, this is quite the opposite of the forced mind control hypnotic state that the Kingdom of darkness keeps its victims in. We have the mind of Christ.

CHAPTER NINE

Worship Metamorphoses and Transfigures the Worshipper

As stated time and again in this book, worshipping the Lord Jesus Christ as a lifestyle is imperative. We are changed from glory to glory as we worship. We have less of us and the corruption of this world and more of Jesus to shine out from our lives. God knows exactly which principality and power is operating in a particular area and what they are trying to accomplish within whatever period of time. It may be for example to bring poverty to an area to prevent the church from advancing. As the Body of Christ worship Jesus in His providing nature (Jehovah Jireh) He shows us where our provision is and because we have His nature we are transformed into generous givers of his gifts to the poor. People see a faithful providing God using His generous servants to minister to them and are drawn to the Lord. They are born into the kingdom of God and come into a relationship with God as they are led to repentance and conversion to Christianity. The work of the principality is thus frustrated because a superior power that works the opposite of greed and poverty has successfully overcome them.

Worship transfigures you into the type of person God can effectively use as His instrument in a particular situation. We must worship our way into the miraculous and the supernatural that we are naturally super. Our worship must be able to heal the sick and raise the dead. Worship sends sound waves into the atmosphere that causes shifts in the elements---wind, air, water and fire. Worship then is divine cosmic energy that cannot be stopped or return void. It's just like the Word of God, it shall not return void unto Me but shall accomplish that which I please says the Lord. (Isaiah 55:11) KJV

With this persistent transformation of our beings we can literally change the atmosphere around our homes, neighborhoods, job environments etc. We can literally become light that displaces darkness. Demons of darkness flee from the light of Jesus in us when we enter any building, place etc. We are clothed in garments of righteousness and light and bring His sweet aroma to distil that which pollutes and poisons. Our very speech is so anointed as a natural outflow of whom we are abiding in that people just hunger and thirst for what we have---the marvelous gift of worship as we remain united with Christ. God can literally purify and cleanse the places we dwell in as He lives His Life through us.

The issue of how to balance our lives to accommodate a worshipping lifestyle now arises. How do we live in the theophany of the Presence of God as He wills?. We have to develop a place and space for Him on a regular basis. Jesus did this as our pattern example. The scriptures record that He would often resort to a quiet place away from the crowds and their incessant demands. Jesus was often exhausted after His daily ministrations to the crowds who thronged Him every day. He was hungry, tired and wearied by the attitudes of the scoffers and mockers. But He knew Who had called Him. He knew his source of strength and power. He knew where to go and have His theophany with God the Father. Therefore He was never defeated on any occasion. He knew the awesome balance He would have and maintain by dwelling in theophanic constantly. He said "I do nothing except My Father first reveal it to Me (John 5:19 KJV). Thus He could be transformed or transfigured at God's will.

Need we expect anything less? Certainly not! We are all fearfully and wonderfully made and peculiarly wired for intelligent worship of our Creator on a daily basis. We have to stop limiting ourselves to the idea that worshipping is just singing songs or making noise. Worship is much far much more than that. We worship by our walk, our speech, our behavior, our decisions everything we do as we live and breathe the breath of life. For in Him we live and move and have our being—thus in Him we live and worship and have our being (Acts 17:28 KJV). The Psalmist exclaims—'Oh that my ways were directed to keep thy statutes (Psalm 119:5. KJV) This is an exceedingly great insight into our pursuit of worshipping God. It brings an immediate relief to stop comparing and competing with each other as this is one of the reasons we are so unbalanced as worshippers.

One of the many benefits of being metamorphosed in worship is that we cease to be burdened by the opinions of others. For us to be strategic in spiritual warfare this is a costly hazard. Our upbringing has made us so performance oriented that we always feel we have to do something to get God moving. However, God is more interested in us being someone, or have a certain posture and attitude for Him to live His Life through us. Worshipping God helps us to be our real selves consistently and to overcome the temptation to be men-pleasers. This enables us invariably to resist the devil. Thus we overcome the world the flesh and the devil (2 Corinthians 4:4). For all that is of the world, the flesh and the devil will pass away, but he that doeth the will of the Father shall abide forever. To do the will of the Father one must know the will of the Father and to know the will one must be a sincere worshipper.

Being transfigured helps us to do warfare most effectively. Imagine going into the camp of the enemy (as often as we must do to take back what was stolen) and we look so much like Jesus that the demons believe its Jesus Himself who is there and hands over the goods "without firing a single shot 'as we would say. This is done all the time in such awesome fear of God the demons beg to go into the swine (or whatever they wish) just to flee immediately from the believer. We have also heard time and again that we must be free from sin to enter the camp of the enemy. We also know It is highly important to be heavily armed with the armor of God and full of the anointing. However, we must also bear Christ image so startlingly that the principalities and powers cannot know the difference-they just flee at once. This requires the theophany like Jesus transfiguration. His garments gleamed so brightly and His countenance was so full of light it would have blinded and killed any enemy in sight. The atmosphere was so charged the disciples slept in deep slumber.

Elijah had the greatest theophany even before Christ entry to the earth. He was taken up in a chariot to heaven. His worship and warfare made such a difference he was not only transfigured, he was translated. This could never have happened with just a casual worship experience or a few battles in the camp of the enemy. Elijah lived a life separated unto the pursuit of God. He chased after God. He pursued his present presence. We must learn not to camp out at a particular place of revelation and make it a monument. Rather, we must pursue God with a passion to where He actually is. An up to date and fresh revelation prevents spiritual backsliding and inertia.

We must not however discard the previous revelation as this is a boost to our faith when we contending in a fresh battle with the enemy. Elijah had just seen the slaughter of 450 prophets of Baal. He had just witnessed the awesome power of God dry up all the water in the trenches of sacrifice (1Kings 19: 1-14 KJV) Yet when he heard the threats of Jezebel he ran for his life, sat under a juniper tree and requested that he should die. Fear and exhaustion were the real weapons of the enemy Jezebel. This principality has this specific assignment—to destroy the prophets of God. If God could destroy all those prophets consuming them with fire, surely one railing witch would be nothing to deal with. God in His mercy refreshes Elijah (1 Kings 19: 5—8 KJV)

Nevertheless, Elijah's exploits for God were so awesome that he was able to give a double portion of his anointing to Elisha the younger prophet. We must do the greater works as the Body of Christ in these last few days. Knowing the principality by name, its assignment, weapons and devices allows us a greater insight for strategic warfare. The prophetic ministry like all Body gifts must be undergirded with twenty four hour daily prayer, praise and worship. The weapons of intimidation, exhaustion and suicidal depression must be rendered permanently powerless with the high praises of God. David built a tent in his backyard for the Ark of God and paid people fulltime to worship before the Lord. We cannot take the city with Friday Night Prayer Meeting alone with some fasting here and there. It's a dedicated year round worship battalion of intercessors who will break the gates of bronze and iron. This can be done on a shift and rotational basis.

Interestingly enough, JP Timmons points out that all the principalities and powers meet for an all night meeting the last Friday of every month. The Body of Christ needs to take note. There are several ministries who have a prayer watch for 30 days and pray for different requests. However, the level of preparation for worship transfiguration and theophanic interaction with God and angels from His throne is much higher than what presently obtains. This is where God's Spirit carries you from place to place in the spirit realm as He wills just as He did with so many of His prophets. The Word of the Lord (especially in the Old Testament) declares---"The Spirit of the Lord carried me away--------- etc. Regardless of the level of counterfeit operations of this nature that is perpetrated in the Kingdom of Darkness, the genuine move of the Holy Spirit to use God's people supernaturally cannot be ignored or stopped. The true and genuine will prevail because the work of Jesus Christ on the Cross cannot and will never be nullified.

CHAPTER TEN

Why We Must Contend for Worship of the Godhead

It is worth reminding ourselves as members of the Body of Christ that the battle belongs to the Lord at all times and at all levels. However, at this level of warfare in the second heaven IT IS ABSOLUTELY IMPERATIVE THAT WE BE LED OF THE LORD AGAINST THESE POWERS. WE MUST GET HIS SPECIFIC ORDERS, APPROVAL AND DIRECTION TO ENGAGE THE ENEMY AT THIS LEVEL. WE MUST GUARD AGAINST PRIDE IN PARTICULAR AND THE DESIRE TO GRANDSTAND OUR GIFTINGS ETC. This is why books such as these although printed now have a specific time when they will be activated by THE LORD JESUS CHRIST HIMSELF. Failure to adhere to these warnings will result in "needless casualties of war' as pointed out by John Paul Jackson (in his book with the same name) and so many others. It is a preparation manual for events in the near future. It is to make us aware of the strategy of the enemy and to help us to RESIST THE DEVIL right up to the time just before the

Lord's return when God will appoint special high ranking angels under the Chief Warrior Angel Michael. They themselves will do the fighting for us as they prepare us to really withstand just before the RAPTURE.

In the second heaven the principalities and powers direct the worship of satanists via numerous methods, such as horoscope readings of the 12 zodiac signs, manipulation of the planets, sun, moon and stars etc. For example, those who worship the moon inadvertently are worshipping the moon goddess Ashtaroth and those who worship the sun worship the sun god known as Ra or Baal. and other names This entire region is busy day and night connecting those in spiritual wickedness in high places (the Satanists, witches, free masons illuminati rosicrucians, magicians) etc on the earth with this second heaven. The leylines, pulleys, sacred geometry and scientific devices, astral and psychic channeling etc are used incessantly to keep the communication going.

When believers pray, worship and seek to communicate with the true and living God in heaven (called the third heaven) these are the forces that resist us on earth as well as God's angels from His throne when they are sent to our assistance. The conflict is total. It's called wrestling----"For we wrestle not against flesh and blood but against principalities and powers, rulers of darkness (Ephesians 6:10. KJV) For our prayers to get pass these to God in heaven we have to put on the Whole Armor Of God and contend forcefully only with the help of angels. There is no other way out. They are like roadblocks but praise God the weapons of our warfare are not carnal but mighty through God to the pulling down of strongholds (2 Corinthians 10:4 KJV) and we overcome him by the Blood of the Lamb and the word of our testimony (Rev: 12:11 KJV)

Our faith as believers does not rest on the religious, political systems of this world. We trust in the One who has conquered this world by the finished work of the Cross. We have been mandated by God to fight the good fight of faith, to have our senses rightly exercised in the business of the kingdom of God. Before coming to the saving knowledge of Jesus Christ we all had our conversation in this world (behavior, lifestyles etc) which was contrary to God. We were therefore alienated from God and the true worship of the Godhead (Colossians 1:21 KJV). Our parents, ancestors and the entire human race were in this condition. All have sinned and come short of the glory of God (Romans 3:23 KJV). Our new found faith in God through the atoning work of Christ Cross informs us that there is a fight to fight. That is why we need this faith.

The Book of Jude depicts a horrendous struggle or contention for the faith. This is because damnable heresies have crept into the church and the teachings of Christ are in danger of mixture if we do not contend for the faith. The only way to contend effectively for this faith is to be so transfigured in worship to bear Christ image fully that lies cannot stand in our presence. There is such a righteous and earnest glory in the life of the worshippers we actually repel the negative energy that surrounds the lies. The Word of God in our mouths is the Word that comes out of His mouth and it swings every which way. The Psalmist says "the voice of the Lord will shatter the enemy with His scepter He will strike them down" (Isaiah 27:7, 2 KJV Corinth 10: 5 KJV)

The plan of the enemy is to use these lies and heresies to nullify the worship of Jesus in the Godhead. He knows how important worship is in creating a desired image, attitude and lifestyle of a person. All those who are born again begin to enjoy the wonderful depths and heights of worship. They are enthralled but most of all they are changed into what the whole creation and earth is groaning for---the manifestation of the sons of God. After the fall of Lucifer, and 1/3 of the angels, the earth went into convulsions of catastrophe. The earth was never designed for this but to worship the Creator. God had to make a new earth (Genesis 1:1-2 KJV) and form Adam from the dust of the new earth. Of course Adam's fall led to the groaning of this new earth again.

The final groaning of the earth will end when Jesus Christ returns and establishes a new heaven and a new earth for His Church Bride. At last His image is formed in mankind through the finished work of the Cross. And it's all accomplished by the contending for the worship of the Godhead. Now having formed His image in us, we His worshippers now choose Him and His Righteousness over our own sinful fallen nature. We choose to abide in His ways, His Truth and His Life. We are worshippers of Him for all eternity. According as He hath chosen us before the foundation of the earth, our souls cry out, 'Even so, come Lord Jesus fashion us your way even as you were fashioned to be the Last Adam from the beginning. You O Lord are the Last Adam---a quickening Spirit, so quicken us Dear Lord Jesus Christ.

Our worship must pierce the darkness even as Jesus' body was pierced for us on the Cross. Believers are deceived (because of the old Adamic nature) that we feel we have to reserve continuous praise of God for when we get to heaven. We are made to feel that worship is out of place on the earth. So we have a postponement mentality—in the sweet bye and bye. This is a total lie from the Kingdom of darkness because Jesus taught in the Lord's Prayer---Thy Kingdom come on earth as it is in heaven' Righteousness,

Peace, Joy in the Holy Ghost that's the Kingdom of God on earth because that's already in heaven. This is only possible with the theophanic type of worship that so metamorphoses us that the principalities and powers that rule over earth's families, health, education, sports, politics, jurisprudence, military etc are disarmed.

We are constantly graduating in God's school of worship to possess our land. The level of worship we experienced when we were first born again was just a scratch on the surface. Deep calleth unto deep at the noise of thy waterspouts (Psalm 42:7 KJV) We pray and fast for long periods with little effect (our government, health, education systems remain the same) Since Christ is the Head of all principality and power He must be the Head in all our earthly human systems as well. In Him dwelleth all the fullness of the Godhead bodily and we are complete in Him(Colossians 2: 10) If in Him we live and move and have our being then in Him we must contend for worship of the Godhead by dismantling the enemy's stronghold from our nation and our worship and turn both over to God.

The Man-child Company spoken of in Revelation 12:5 KJV are God's End Time Generals who will literally ascend to god's throne even as Elijah did. Where Jesus is there we are also. The Beast System of the New World Order requires the triple six mark in the head or hand to buy and sell. People will use this as a device to activate bank accounts etc in a cashless and cardless society. Already we see what science/technology has implemented in the form of automatic doors in stores and banks which just swing open when you stand in front of them. We are not going to be around for these terrible events. That's why we need to be part of the Man-child Company (so metamorphosed we are raptured away in His presence). He said in His Word---Let us pray that we be counted worthy to escape these things (Luke 21: 36 KJV)

The great necessity of being metamorphosed cannot be overemphasized. We cannot just say---'I plead the Blood of Jesus' and stop there. Divine power and virtue must be so imbedded in us things begin to come to order in our presence. We move from the Moses posture (the Written Word) and Elijah (the Spoken Word) to Jesus (the Manifested Word). This is depicting Moses, Elijah and Jesus in the Transfiguration. Note it was the Mount of Transfiguration not the Valley or Plain of Transfiguration. It implies a climbing up higher in order to be changed. It calls for really pressing forward to the mark of the high calling in Jesus. We cannot remain where we are and be changed.

Numerous demonized symbols permeate our world that requires us not only to be discerning but to contend for worship of the Godhead. When we examine the origin of the double snake wrapped on a cross as the logo symbol of the oath of the medical field---it dates back to ancient Greek mythology (it's the magic wand of the Greek god Hermes/Mercury messenger of gods, conductor of the dead) Instead of promoting vitality and health as befits the [4]medical field it means temporality, perishableness and senility.

Power must change hands says David Olikuyo as he rightfully points out the need to forcefully and violently seize what rightfully belongs to us. All his prayers are so designed. The Kingdom of Heaven suffereth violence since the days of John the Baptist and the violent taketh it by force (Matthew 11:12 KJV). We the Body of Christ who are born in the end times must see our presence on earth at this

---

[4] David Olukoya, Power Must Change Hands (Lagos: tracts and publication Group, 2010) pgs 1-20

time as very prophetic. We are the generation that will see the RETURN OF THE LORD ON EARTH. We must go into the enemy's camp and take back what he stole from us. Indeed power must change hands as we withstand in these last evil days.

CHAPTER ELEVEN

How We Must Contend for Effective End Time Worship

We know from the scriptures that the RAPTURE OF THE CHURCH must and will take place. No flesh would remain alive without the rapture---it's the time of Jacob's trouble(Jeremiah 30: 4-7,Daniel 12: 1, Amos 5: 18 KJV). Whether the Rapture will take place before or during the Tribulation is still not 100% certain but what we do know is that it will take place. The Beast System as predicted in the book of Revelation will rise up in a one world government led by the anti-christ. The mark of the Beast will be instituted as no buying or selling can be done without it. However, the life of the Church must have been preceded by how a thorough working knowledge of how worshipping the Lord Jesus Christ can displace the principalities and powers. This valuable tried and tested experience gives the Body of Christ the valuable tools and weapons necessary to really withstand in the last days.

Only the major principalities and Powers will be used as examples here as many of the lesser powers are not mentioned specifically by name in the Bible but come under the general category of evil demonic powers and spirits. The example of Legion in the man in the graveyard is an example of over 6,000 demons living in one person. Their specific names were not given as Jesus dealt with them as one single group casting all out at once. JP Timmons book –Mysterious secrets of the Dark Kingdom pages 99-199 gives the name of each one and their assignment which he discovered after helping to deliver several souls from this kingdom and they disclosed their names. This shows us clearly that God uses His Word to reveal their names as well as the experiences of those persons in the Body of Christ who have been exposed to the battleground of deliverance for many years

It is very, very, very important that the following conditions prevail in all such meetings by the Body of Christ to deal with these principalities, powers and spiritual hosts in the second heaven. Proper teaching of the names, assignments of each.

A) The Lord Jesus Christ Himself must authorize, ordain and approve the decision to go up against these principalities, powers and spiritual hosts in the second heaven.

B) It is always a group that goes up not for lone rangers at all.

C) According to JP Timmons a minimum of three and maximum of seven pastors who have prayed and fasted before and at least one must be an accurate prophet. They should take Communion also. The rest of the congregation must repent as well.

D) These pastors and prophets will be in charge of the meeting and as led of the Lord.

E) The pastors, prophets must petition the Lord to send the angels to do the binding and loosing of these principalities and powers and spiritual hosts in the Second Heaven. IT IS AGAINST SPIRITUAL PROTOCOL TO DO SO ON YOUR OWN IN THE SECOND HEAVEN.

F) There must be no sin and especially no major sin in anyone especially the leaders

G) This is why even before the actual battle begins a final repentance is done

The model presented here is not a fixed and or rigid system to follow but rather a general guideline. We must ensure that we are crucified with Christ to do this level of warfare. As stated earlier, worshipping Jesus in a particular aspect of His nature and character helps to meet our need. An illustration to use this against the principalities and powers will suffice here. In chapter 6 we see that the principality Apollyon is mainly responsible for political systems of the world. He is helped by Baal and Ashtaroth. The Body of Christ must know which Zodiac Sign the area is linked to and only with the leading of the Lord we petition God to send His warring Angels to blot out all programming in that star sign and to bind that principality, power, or spiritual hosts and their subservient spirits and activities and to loose the right and necessary spirits to replace those evil ones.

ILLUSTRATION: WAR IN THE HEAVENLIES AGAINST APOLLYON [POLITICS]

The Lord may commission and lead a group of Holy Ghost filled pastors/prophets to go up against the principality Apollyon because the political leaders of a region may want to pass same sex laws and marriages which the church must stand against.

Scriptures: All King James Version KJV Job 26:6, Job 28;22, Job 31:12, Psalm 88:11, Proverbs 15:11

Repentance;

Father God we come to you in the name of your Son Jesus our Lord and Saviour seeking your mercy and forgiveness for ourselves and our ancestors for being involved with this principality Apollyon. We ask your cleansing and healing with the Blood of Jesus. We decree and declare that we are no longer in league with this power as we fully renounce it in its entirety. We join in agreement with our pastors and prophets as they petition you to send angelic assistance in this battle against APOLLYON.

Binding and Loosing (Pastors and prophets petition God to send warring angels to assist)

Father God in the Mighty Name of Jesus Christ we ask you to send your warring and ministering spirits to bind Apollyon, all its activities and all subservient spirits. Strip them of their assignments to influence the laws of our parliament for same sex marriages. We are against this O God even as you are. We ask Dear God that you loose spirits of the fear of the Lord to choose and enforce heterosexuality and natural affections in marriage in passing these laws governing marriage. We come into agreement with you God and decree and declare that there shall be no same sex marriage laws passed in our Parliament.

Songs: Psalm 150-----KJV-

-Let the high praises be in our mouths, And a two-edged sword in our hand
To execute the vengeance of our God and the judgment that's written

Song: Let us rejoice and be glad giving the glory to Him. For the marriage of the Lamb has come. And the bride has made herself ready

Song: I will extol your love more than wine, Draw me after you and let us run together, I will extol your love more than wine.

WAR IN THE HEAVENLIES AGAINST ABADDON (Eternal Destruction)]

Abaddon means Eternal Destruction just like Apollyon but their functions are different. Abaddon is a tall, black and foul smelling demon, often when ministering to homosexuals, a minister can smell his presence. He is called –THE Polluting Demon. He is in charge of polluting and corrupting habits such as smoking cocaine and other drugs, rock music, pornography, homosexuality, fornication, incest, bestialiy, pedophilia and alcohol abuse and adultery. He raised up many discotheques to encourage sexual immorality. He was responsible for inventing the strobe light. He is behind rock music with altar calls to accept satan. Don't allow your teenagers to go to these rock concerts, many are not really aware of what it all means— giving their lives to satan. The same is true of Christian rap and rock music]

Scriptures: Proverbs 27: 20, KJV Revelation 9:11 KJV

Repentance;

Father God we are truly sorry for being involved in sexual sins controlled by Abaddon and all other related sins this demon ensnares people into. We ask your mercy, forgiveness deliverance and cleansing from all these sins. Your Word declares our bodies are the temples of The Lord and that you will destroy all those who defile the body. We ask that the Blood of Jesus be applied to all areas of our lives affected by these sins and we pledge never to go back to them knowing that destruction will surely follow such willful disobedience. Thank you Father for your unfailing mercy in Jesus Name. We come into agreement with our pastors and prophets as they petition You to send angelic assistance in this battle against Abaddon.

Binding and Loosing;
Pastors and prophets petition God to send warring and ministering angels to bind Abaddon with fetters of iron and to command a cessation to its activities in the lives of those concerned. They ask god to loose spirits of the fear of the Lord concerning sexual purity, abstinence, self control and faithfulness in the marital relations, home and family.

Songs
Any suitable songs can be sung and as the Lord leads

WAR IN THE HEAVENLIES AGAINST BELIAL [War and Death]

This principality causes war and death. He is the same as an evil worthless person. He works with Magog—the god of war
Scriptures: All King James Version KJV 2 Corinth 6;15, Deut 13:13, 1 Sam 1:16, 1 Sam 2:12, Judges 19:22, 20:13

Repentance
Father God we repent of causing war and death in any way among the nations, especially if in any way in ignorance we caused this against the nation of Israel. We ask your

mercy and forgiveness and pledge that we will only take your leading in this matter if and/or when it arises.

Binding and Loosing

Pastors and prophets petition God to send His angels to bind Belial and all servient spirits and their activities of war and death in the lives concerned and to loose spirits of peace and goodwill among the nations. Pray for God's wisdom in the government and spiritual leadership of the land.

Songs

Any appropriate song can be added here and as the Lord leads

WAR IN THE HEAVENLIES AGAINST THE BEAST (666)

Jesus is the Lamb of God which takes away the sins of the world. The opposite nature of a lamb is a beast, cruel, merciless in intent and action. Yet Jesus the Lion of the tribe of Judah is exalted over the Beast. As we give the Lord Lion and Lamb worship we overcome the Beast. Hallelujah

Scriptures; Revelation 13:17, KJV Revelation 14: 9—11, KJV Revelation 20: 4 KJV

Repentance:

Father God we repent on behalf of ourselves and our ancestors of worshipping the Beast and his system by following after materialism, love of money and the whole business system of the world. Our god was our belly and the pursuit of money our goal at the expense of trusting in your Word and being contented there with. We know from your Word that this principality will work to force men to accept the mark of the Beast during the time of the

Tribulation. If the righteous scarcely be saved where shall the ungodly appear? We humbly beseech thee Dear Lord to have mercy and forgive us this sin of greed, love of money, mammon, worldliness. Wash and cleanse us from this sin as we renounce it utterly. We come into agreement with our pastors and prophets as they petition You to send angelic assistance in this battle against THE BEAST

Binding and Loosing [pastors and prophets petition God to send angels to assist]

Father God we petition you to send warring and ministering spirits bind the Beast and all subservient spirits and their assignments to control us through the love of money through the business world. We ask you to loose spirits of godliness with contentment, free enterprise, fair play, true balances and monetary justice. We decree and declare that we will live by these principles until the return of Christ Jesus.

Songs;

a) The Lion of the tribe of Judah has broken every chain
b) Victory Chant—Hail Jesus You are My King

WAR IN THE HEAVENLIES AGAINST LEVIATHAN (PRIDE)

Scriptures: All King James Version KJV
Prov: 6;17, Prov:16:18, Job 41, Psalm 74; 14 Isaiah 27:1,Rev 12: 1-17, Gen 1: 20-23, Rev 22:1-2

Reflective meditative worship of Jesus as the Personification of Humility must be done to displace pride and Leviathan. According to Amanda Buys in her book— The Four Elements Leviathan has several heads [Pleides,

Alnitak, Betelgeuse, Bellatrix, Mintaka, Alnilam, Rigel, Saiph Worshippers may feel pain in the shoulders as pride lives in all human beings. Leviathan fights the gifts of the Holy Spirit in the Holy of Holies. People with the gifts of the Holy Spirit may be manipulated by this spirit with a) shyness or b) pride and boasting especially if they were once involved in Freemasonry etc.

Repentance
Father in the Faithful Name of the Lord Jesus Christ, we come to you for your Mercy, Forgiveness deliverance and healing from the spirit of Pride. We recognize that this is an innate tendency of the human race to walk in pride since the fall of mankind. The scriptures warn of the pride of life, our pride in material things, achievements at the expense of our relationship with you and the destiny of our souls. You resist the proud dear Lord but give Grace to the humble. Teach us how to humble ourselves daily in all our activities and relationships for in due season you will exalt the humble and the meek but overthrow the mighty from their seat. We petition You now to send your mighty angels of war to do battle against this principality and set us free in Jesus Name. Amen.

Binding and Loosing
Pastors and prophets petition God to send His angels to do battle against this spirit of Pride/ Leviathan, to dry up its waters and to render it powerless to operate in our lives. Ask God to loose spirits of humility upon us and that we be clothed in humility at all times.

Songs
Any suitable song/songs can be sung here

WAR IN THE HEAVENLIES AGAINST ASHTAROTH
(False Religions)

Our worship of God against this principality must come in alignment with Jesus Nature as the only way to God. This principality is responsible for deceiving the races of mankind that there are many roads to God and it doesn't matter which religion you are born into or hail from, it's alright you can still serve God. This we know is false and the church cannot condone its members trying to serve God and at the same time practicing the religion of their culture. A Hindu for example cannot continue to make puja sacrifices to his various gods such as Shiva, Brahma, Kali Mai etc and at the same time attend a Christian church, be baptized or even take communion. Some people are so fearful of severing these ties with their past ancestral religions that they secretly continue to serve them while outwardly seeming to serve Christ. Likewise the Muslim, Buddhist, Sikh etc cannot have an altar at home burning incense to their idols and hope to become a Christian by attending church. Even the Roman Catholic believer who repeats several Hail Mary's and bows to statues of "saints" is in complete error to the truth of the Gospel. Ashtaroth is in charge of all these false religions and must be identified by name specifically (as well as all the other principalities and powers) by the church leaders and be bound by the angels of God in the second heaven. Ashtaroth works with Apollyon and Baal. They are the heads of all religious spirits. Whenever Ashtaroth is on the earth (According to Amanda Buys in her book—The Four Elements) she dwells under the black stone at the most holy shrine of Islam located in Mecca in Saudi Arabia. She is also known as:

a) Diane of the Ephesians
b) Venus or Rhea
c) Isis
d) Is of India
e) Shang Mao
f) Irene
g) Holy Mary
h) Queen of the Heaven

Scriptures: Revelation 11: 15, KJV Jeremiah 7:18 KJV, Jeremiah 44:17, 19,25 KJV

Repentance:
Father God we repent on behalf of ourselves and our ancestors for being involved in false religion headed by this principality. We renounce these idols, beliefs and practices and turn to you with all of our hearts, souls and minds to worship The Lord Jesus Christ only as God Almighty and promise to serve no other. We ask your Mercy, forgiveness deliverance and healing all involvement with this entity. Thank you for all this in Jesus Name. Amen.

Binding and Loosing
The pastors and prophets petition God to send warring angels to bind this principality and all servient spirits and their activities in their lives and to loose spirits of the truth, doctrines of the truth in God's Word, discernment and revelation knowledge of the Kingdom of God and His Christ.

Songs
Any suitable songs can be sung here and as the Lord leads

WAR IN THE HEAVENLIES AGAINST BAAL [OCCULTISM]

[5]Raising the altar of the Lord Jesus Christ over all altars of Baal and thanking God for the Blood of His Son Jesus Christ is a good way of overcoming the presence and activities of Baal in our worship of the Lord Jesus Christ. This is especially important in areas where sacrifices including human sacrifices are made by heathen worshippers of the cults of Baal.

We all know the story of Elijah and the prophets of Baal who were noted for cutting themselves (1 Kings 18: 28)as they vainly called upon their god Baal to answer by fire and consume the sacrifice in the contest. Israel had angered the Lord by their involvement with Baal (the bull god) similar to that of the Hindus. JP Timmons in his book---Mysterious secrets of the Dark Kingdom page 114 notes this about Baal:

a) Baal is the power worshipped by the Canaanites
b) Known as the Sun God, works with Ashtaroth and Apollyon to promote false religion
c) Introduced the OCCULT
d) The children of Israel worshipped Baal when they worshipped the Golden Calf
e) Enjoys sacrifice of the first born done as a mockery to God and the Passover
f) Taught mankind the hypnotic and psychological effects of light. Helped to develop the lighting effects used in discotheques today as heavy rock metal music

---

[5]   JP Timmons, Mysterious Secrets of the Dark Kingdom (Manchaca: CCI Publishing 1991) pg 114

g) Possessed Nebuchadnezzar during his insanity

h) His name means star or sun, Third Eye, Star of Lucifer

Scriptures: All King James Version KJV- Jeremiah 19: 5, Hosea 2: 17, Judges 2: 11, Judges 10: 10, 1 Kings 18:18, Exodus

1Kings 16:30–33

Repentance:

Father God we come to you seeking your forgiveness, mercy, deliverance and healing for any involvement we and our ancestors have had with this demonic entity—Baal the god of blood and insanity. We denounce and renounce this power as wicked and evil and cast it out of our lives. We repent of all blood sins connected with this spirit including abortion, murders, blood sacrifices etc and thank you Lord for your deliverance for us and our generations.

Binding and Loosing

All pastors and prophets will petition God to send warring and ministering angels to bind Baal and all servient spirits in the heavenlies so that its activities are rendered powerless and inoperative. They request that God loose spirits of life, sanity, the sacredness of life, peace and wellbeing upon all present

WAR IN THE HEAVENLIES AGAINST GOG AND MAGOG (WAR)

Most terrorist activities are undergirded by this power. The Muslim Jihads, and Isis groups which behead people are typical examples of what needs to be bound in Jesus Mighty

Name. The full magnitude of Psalm 91, the whole armor of God, the help of warring and ministering angels must accompany our worship experience against Gog and Magog. For this reason, Michael the chief warrior angel of heaven is usually deployed to help the nation of Israel to prevail in battle. Since the Body of Christ is spiritual Israel we must align ourselves with all God's Covenant blessings for Israel [Exodus 23:22]—I will be an enemy to your enemy and an adversary to your adversary. JT TIMMON states these facts about these powers:

a) Magog is the power and demon of war. Works closely with the white witches in the design and manufacture of war weapons, equipment and technology.

b) Has a spiritual laboratory where thousands of demons and some humans do research night and day to develop new technology and weapons designed to wage war and kill. The demons are not concerned with who wins the war but only that blood is shed.

c) All the witches work with him to make war—white, black and red witches

d) Works with Belial and use servient spirits to stir up war—spirits of hate, anger and fear. These work with 13 other spirits including unforgiveness. This triplet spirit can exercise tremendous control over a person causing them to kill and then wonder why they did it.

e) Gog is the guardian spirit over Germany. In World War 111 Germany will attack Israel—Battle of Armageddon –Ezekiel 38, 39 KJV

f) Magog is the Guardian spirit over China and the Soviet Union (Russia)

Scriptures: Ezekiel 38, Ezekiel 39, Psalm 46: 9

Repentance:

Father God we come to you in the Name of your Son Jesus Christ to repent of any and all sins we and our ancestors have committed by being involved with these powers and being guilty of anti-Semitism by supporting wars against Israel. We declare healing and restoration to the nation of Israel

Binding and Loosing

All pastors and prophets petition God to send warring and ministering spirits to bind Gog and Magog and all servient spirits in the heavenlies and cause wars to cease unto the ends of the earth. They ask that spirits of world peace be loosed and healing flow to all those affected especially the nation of Israel

Songs Any suitable songs can be sung here and as the Lord leads

1) Victory Chant—hail Jesus you're my king, your life frees me to sing
2) The Lord is a Man of War
3) You are exalted Lord above all else

WAR IN THE HEAVENLIES AGAINST PAIMON (FORTUNE TELLING, FAMILIAR SPIRITS)

This power controls all celestial or heavenly demons. He is involved in the heavens and has influence over the stars and planets. He works with Baal or Orion and Belial since Belial is over the planets and stars. He speaks to people through mirrors, crystal balls and water. He is lord over soothsayers and fortune tellers and introduces himself as Michael the archangel. People can learn the history of any living person living on the earth by looking into these magic mirrors. The spirit pretends to be the Voice of God to fool people, provides false prophesy with the use of familiar spirits.

Scriptures: I Samuel KJV

Saul consults the witch of Endor

The same pattern of repentance binding and loosing should be done with this demonic entity. Similarly all relevant songs that apply to counter the work of this power should be sung

Songs
Any suitable song can be sung here and as the Lord leads

WAR IN THE HEAVENLIES AGAINST BEELZEBUB (EVERYTHING THAT FLIES---WITCHES, WIZARDS AEROPLANES ETC)

This power controls everything that flies [aero planes, all demons, witches, wizards] It is known as one of the bodyguards of satan. Establishing the Lordship of Jesus Christ in the heavenlies is highly important here. The Bible calls satan the prince of the power of the air and Beelzebub as the prince of demons. These are some facts about him.

a) His name means Lord of the Flies as he controls all that flies
b) He is in charge of collecting blood sacrifices of witches and wizards made to satan
c) Like all the other higher order demons he only feeds on blood (human blood)

d) Witches and wizards kill people through witchcraft or remote control—the Class 111 witches are called Alpha and Omega Order

e) Class 111 witches are addicted to and feed only on human blood

f) Class 1 witches eat human flesh only

g) They have very large blood banks in the heavens where the blood is taken and stored in reservoirs as large as the size of a Petroleum Refinery

h) He is the specialist in catastrophic destruction and loss of life, accidents, aero plane crashes

Scriptures: All King James Version KJV Mark 3: 20-30, Matthew 12: 22-37, Luke 11: 15

Repentance:

Father God we come to you seeking your forgiveness wherever we and our ancestors have been involved with this demon via witchcraft, necromancy, fortune telling etc. We renounce this power and pledge never to become involved with it again. Thank you Lord for your Mercy, healing and deliverance from this evil spirit.

Binding and Loosing

The pastors and prophets petition God to send warring and ministering angels to bind Beelzebub and all servient spirits strike them with deafness, dumbness and blindness breaking their communication lines and rendering all their activities null and void in this place and over their lives. The angels must also silence the 12 zodiac signs and separate them from Beelzebub cutting off all backlash and retaliation, accident and incident. The angels must also help to loose spirits of security, protection, guardian angels etc over the area and lives involved.

Songs:

a) Let us go up and take the country
b) Any suitable songs can be sung here and as the Lord leads

WAR IN THE HEAVENLIES AGAINST ASHMODEE (POLLUTING DEMON)

This is the main power that causes all pollution especially sexual pollution. It is called the STINKER (a foul smelling demonic looking man). He is tall in stature and walks very lightly with a spring in his step. He has wings like Beelzebub. His main assignments include:

a) Sexual immorality (masturbation, fornication, adultery, incest, oral sex, anal sex, lesbianism, homosexuality, bisexuality, bestiality, pedophilia, pornography, prostitution) all forms of perversion.
b) Marries people for satan, has sex with them
c) Responsible for Jezebel and often works with Baal
d) Causes marital problems [divorce, contempt for one's spouse, marital conflict, miscarriage, death of children

Scriptures: Any suitable scriptures can be used here and as led of the Lord

Repentance:
Father God we come to you repenting of any of these sins we and our ancestors have committed. We renounce

these as evil and sinful and we break ranks with all spirits associated with these sins. These are an abomination to you and we therefore forsake these and warn others to do so. As Jehovah Mekedesh we ask your cleansing fire and the Blood of Jesus Christ to wash us, purify us and make us totally clean and whole. We thank you dear Lord for these mercies Amen.

Binding and Loosing

The pastors and prophets petition God to send warring and ministering angels to bind Ashmodee and all servient spirits in the heavenlies with fetters of iron rendering their activities totally powerless and loosing spirits of the fear of the Lord pertaining to sexual purity, abstinence, faithfulness in marriage, temperance, natural affection etc. in the lives of the people.

Songs

a) Jehovah Mekedesh You're the one that makes us clean
b) Purify your people O God
c) Blessed are the pure in heart, for they shall see their God

WAR IN THE HEAVENLIES AGAINST ARITON [MAGIC, CHARM]

This power is in charge of all demons and agents involved in magical powers. It has mirrors to see the past and future of any person who looks into the mirror. It has hundreds of different magical charms. Charms do not work in the spiritual world only in the physical world. They are given to gain money, power, sex etc. Charms can be used to:

a) Attract men, women   c) Become an instant millionaire

b) Protect   d) Make people sick

d) Magic mirror to kill only------the person's spirit is summoned into the mirror, their face must appear in that mirror. If they appear and they are seen from the front that person will die physically because from the moment they appear in the mirror, they are dead spiritually. However, if the person appears and turns their back upon the one using the mirror that means they cannot be harmed. They have power over the mirror.

Scriptures: He delivers us from the cunning sleight of men's hands Ephesians 4:14 KJV

He confounds the wisdom of the wise and sends diviners mad (1Corinth 1: 27 KJV)

Repentance:
Father God we repent for ourselves and our ancestors for being involved with this spirit through using magic and charms. We now renounce Ariton and all is servient spirits and ask your forgiveness, mercy and healing from these sins and their effects. We thank you and praise you for all these mercies in Jesus Name. Amen

Binding and Loosing
Pastors and prophets petition God to send warring and ministering angels to bind Ariton and all servient spirits rendering their activities powerless in Jesus Name. They ask that spirits of divine revelation knowledge, wisdom and discernment be released in the lives of the people

Songs
Any suitable songs can be sung here and as led of the Lord

WAR IN THE HEAVENLIES AGAINST MAMMON (POVERTY IN CHRISTIANS, GREED, SELFISHNESS)

According to JP Timmons, Mammon occupies the sixth plane above the earth. He is in charge of anything that belongs to satan—his storehouses in the heavenlies, charms, spirits example witchcraft spirits, magic mirrors, fame and many other things. Mammon is a mass merchant and treasurer.

Scriptures: Matthew 6: 24 KJV– Luke 16: 9,13 KJV

Repentance
Father God we repent for ourselves and our ancestors of sins involving money and wealth such as stealing, forgery, not paying our tithes and offerings, tax fraud etc. We ask your forgiveness and mercy as we totally turn away from these sins. O Lord please remove the curse of poverty and lack and send your abundant rain and financial blessing upon us in Jesus Name. We promise not to make wealth our idol but to use it to glorify you and establish your kingdom on earth.

Binding and Loosing
Pastors and prophets petition God to send warring and ministering angels to bind Mammon and all servient spirits in the heavenlies rendering their activities inoperative and loosing spirits of wealth with honor, of contentment, trusting and waiting only on the Lord.

Songs

a) Jehovah Jireh my Provider will supply all my needs
b) Any suitable songs can be sung here and as the Lord leads

The following demonic powers can be dealt with in much the same way as those preceding in the above examples.

Wherever possible scriptures from the King James Version are used here KJV will be given and relevant songs. It must be borne in mind that this is just a pattern or guide not a rigid formula.

WAR IN THE HEAVENLIES AGAINST

MARINE/DAGON	(Mermaid, Merman)1 Samuel 5:2
TINKA	(Replaces human fetus with a snake) Be fruitful and multiply (Gen 1:28 KJV) Children are a heritage from the Lord (Psalm 127: 3 KJV)
DJOKA	(Cripples human spirit)
CYRIEL	(False speaking in tongues)
OGEASO	(Transfers Obanje spirit from Marine to humans making them spirit humans.
ORIONTA	Camelon—helps people assume different spiritual
DJOKA	(Cripples human spirit)
CYRIEL	(False speaking in tongues)

OGEASO	(Transfers Obanje spirit from Marine to humans making them spirit humans.)
ORIONTA	Camelon—helps people assume different spiritual and human forms.
MOLECH	Allows people to let their children pass through Fire, babies as human sacrifices (Scriptures: Leviticus 18, Lev 20: 2,13, Lev: 16 9,13, 1 King 11:7, Jeremiah 32: 35.
ARCARINE	Causes spiritual and natural blindness, uses a spiritual knife.
QUEEN OF THE COAST	Beautiful woman who has a mansion under the sea. She comes to the earth to enlist people for the dark kingdom, promote sexual immorality in the ministry, can assume the form of a man, seen often in Nigeria especially in the East.
THE SPIRITS OF ISLAM	3 Spirits—Majaro, Fregal, Kabah. They work to promote the Islam Faith, work closely with Ashtaroth- Majaro-Holy Jihad, Kabah (Polygamy)
JEZEBEL	A wicked queen who was married to King Ahab. She is assigned to destroy the office of the prophet and she fought against Elijah. The book of Revelation calls her the mother harlots Scriptures: Revelation 2: 20, 2 Kings 9: 22, 2 Kings 9 30--37

CHAPTER TWELVE

Reordering our Day

In light of the preceding chapters we in the Body of Christ recognize that worship of the Lord Jesus Christ is our highest priority. Worship resists the devil indeed and we can be truly seated in heavenly places with Christ Jesus bearing the image of the heavenly. Once the protocols of worshipping Jesus in the Second Heaven are seriously adhered to we can prepare more effectively for Christ Return. Having done all we can stand. We now have the power to reorder our day so that we can join with Christ Jesus to do so and truly say and sing –This is the day that the Lord has made (and we join in cooperation with Him to do so following His leading) we will rejoice and be glad in it.

Reordering our day requires that we in the Body of Christ keep in mind that we were in Christ before the foundation of the earth. Time is a created thing that God created for us to function in and it is divided into different dispensations. We are living in the Day of Christ Resurrection when we can command and demand what is rightfully ours---we do not cry or beg God to do things for us—we can command the blessing. His resurrection permits us who are Blood

Washed and Called Out to live under an Open Heaven. Christ resurrection gives us phenomenal authority. This allows us to reprogram the heavenlies with the Blood of Jesus Christ and the finished work of the Cross as He Leads us to do so. It is always, always, always with His leading and praise He is always willing.

In chapter 11 we see the strategy we can use as an example of how to deal with different principalities and powers to nullify their assignment against us. This means that the day that the Kingdom of Darkness engineered for us cannot manifest. We have the power to decide what type of day we would have as the Body of Christ on earth. Every believer needs to speak the same language and be in one accord as we decree and legislate the Kingdom reign and rule of God over our lives. Of course all this must be accompanied by all out witnessing to the unsaved, praying, fasting, holiness of lifestyle hating and overcoming the world, the flesh and the devil. Think of the awesome power of God as it blows up the strongholds of darkness in the atmosphere as we make our declarations strongly and fearlessly. For example at sunset when God's day begins we as believers can declare the following adhering to all the protocols (petition God to send His angelic hosts etc) and being led by the Lord:

This is the day that the Lord has made, we will rejoice and be glad in it.

We decree and declare that we will live under an open heaven and that the

Sun shall not smite us by day nor the moon by night. We declare that the sun, moon and stars are washed with the Blood of Jesus Christ.

We declare that the planets, especially Venus, Mars, Jupiter, Saturn,

Mercury are all washed with the Blood of Jesus Christ. We decree and declare

That there is a divine silence, deafness, and dumbness among the 12 zodiac

signs and their constellations. We forbid you to speak, we break your

communication lines. We declare that the mercies of God are new every

morning and they will not be hijacked by the enemy. We decree and declare

that the planets will listen to and obey the Voice of the Lord their Creator

and will work for us and not against us. Amen.

We can go on to the days of the week and the months of the year binding the strongman over each, cancelling out their programming and decreeing and declaring God's will instead. In this way we are living directly in the will of God, and being transformed in His image from glory to glory. Amen The heathen meaning of the days of the week and the

months of the year is given by Amanda Buys in her book-
The Four Elements.

PRAYING AGAINST THE HEATHEN
NAMES OF THE DAYS OF THE WEEK
AND MONTHS OF THE YEAR

Days of the Week	Heathen Names of gods and their meanings
Sunday	Sun god— Baal, Ra, pharoah, Caesar
Monday	Moon goddess----Diana, Ashtaroth,
Tuesday	War god---Mars
Wednesday	Magic god -----Mercury
Thursday	Hammer god---Jupiter, Zeus, Torch, Olympic
Friday	Bar-B- Ques/Fish fries------Venus, Isis
Saturday	Wild party/weekends----Saturn, god of agriculture

Months of the Year	Heathen Names of gods and their meanings	Prayers Against Them
January	Date for new magistrates to start. Named After domestic deity called Janus ruler of Beginnings, protector of doorways and And gates and arches	We decree and declare that Janus will not rule in this month-January

February	Female idol Februra	Februra will not Operate in this Month-February
March	Mars—god of war, armies go to war under This diety. Has a chariot with two horses Called Terror and Flight, animals are offered As sacrifice and is called the protector of Vegetation.	This month March will not be ruled by Mars there will be no sacrifice
April	Month of Venus—Great Mother Earth, Lent Mark of Tammuz with ash on Ash Wednesday	This month will not be ruled by Venus, Tammuz
May	God called Maia, daughter of Atlas and One of the 7 sisters of the Pleides	This month will not be ruled by Maia
June	god called Juno— important Roman Female diety, wife and sister of Jupiter Hera Greek Queen of Heaven, Father's Day	This month will not be ruled This month will not be ruled by Juno or the Queen of heaven or the Father's Day Pagan diety
July	Named after Julius Caesar, honored As a deity, son of the sun	This month will not be ruled by the name Julius Caesar

August	Means venerable, awesome Magnificent— Augustus Caesar, Gaius Octavius took this name To honor himself.	This month will not be ruled by the name Augustus Caesar or Gaius Octavious
September	Ruled by Mercury, Mars and Venus By demonic entities operating In these planets.	This month will not be ruled
October	Ruled by Mars, Venus and Pluto	This month will not be ruled by These demons in these planets
November	Ruled by Mars, Jupiter and Pluto	This month will not be ruled By demons in these planets
December	Ruled by Jupiter and Saturn This month will not be ruled By demons in these planets	

The Body of Christ has to blot out all programming in the constellations, the 12 Zodiac signs, all the orbits and circuits and pathways with THE BLOOD OF JESUS CHRIST. Inheritance patterns and cycles must be cancelled and command that the enemy speak no more. The pulleys and connections which pull occultists and connect them to heavenly bodies must be cut [they pull the people back up and reconnect them. The time clock of satan must be smashed especially at birthdays. All these insights must be taken seriously by the Body of Christ if we are to become just like Jesus in the Earth.

There is also the need to RENOUNCE THE 12 ZODIAC SIGNS with relevant scriptures such as outlined by Amanda Buys in her book------The Four Elements. They are as follows

Aries: Mar 21 – April 20----------------Micah 2: 13 –the breaker is coming up before them, they have broken up and have passed through the gate, and are gone out by it and their king shall pass before them, and the Lord on the head of them.

1) Taurus: Apr 2--- May 20----------------1 Chiron 15:27, Nehemiah 8: 10------And David was clothed with a robe of fine linen and all the Levites that bare the ark, and the singers and Chenaniah the master of the song with the singers. David also had upon him an ephod of linen. Neh: 8:10—then he said unto them, Go your way, eat the fat and drink the sweet and send portions for them for whom nothing is prepared: for this day is holy unto our Lord: neither be ye sorry; for the joy of the Lord is your strength

2) Gemini: May 21—Jun 21--------------Isaiah 55:9-11 For as the heavens are higher than the earth, so are my ways higher than your ways, and my thoughts than your thoughts

3) Cancer: June 22---Jul 23----------------John 3:5----Jesus answered, Verily, verily, I say unto thee, except a man be born of water and of the Spirit, he cannot enter into the kingdom of God

4) Leo: July 24---Aug 23-------------Deuteronomy 30:6, Revelation 5; 5-----And the Lord thy God

shall circumcise thine heart and the heart of thy seed, to love the Lord thy God with all thine heart and with all thy soul, that thou mayest live.

5) Virgo: August 24—Sept 23-----Psalm 111;10, Proverbs 6:23------The fear of the Lord is the beginning of wisdom, a good understanding have all they that do his commandments, his praise endureth forever. Proverbs 6:23-----For the commandment is a lamp, and the law is light, and reproofs of instruction are the way of life

6) Libra: Sept 24---Oct 23---------Ephesians 1:7------ In whom we have redemption through his blood, the forgiveness of sins, according to the riches of his grace

7) Scorpio: 24 Oct—Nov 23------Isaiah 25: 8----He will swallow up death in victory, and the Lord God shall wipe away tears from off all their faces, and the rebuke of his people shall he take away from off all the earth, for the Lord hath spoken it

8) Sagittarius: Nov 23-Dec 22----Mark 10:18, Proverbs 19: 2, Isaiah 9:6-----And Jesus answered and said unto him, why callest me good/ there is none good, but one that is God. Prov 19:2—Also that the soul be without knowledge, it is not good, and he that hasteth with his feet sinneth

9) Capricorn: Dec 23---Jan 20----1 John 4:4---Ye are of God little children, and have overcome them; because greater is he that is within you, than he that is within the world.

10) Aquarius: Jan 21---Feb 19------Proverbs 2:6,7---For the Lord giveth wisdom, out of his mouth cometh knowledge and understanding., He layeth up sound

    wisdom for the righteous, he is a buckler to them that walk uprightly

11) Pisces: Feb 20-----Mar 20-------Job 33: 28------He shall deliver his soul from going into the pit, and his life shall see the light.

These signs have to be literally renounced according to the Zodiac sign each Christian and member of the Body of Christ is born under because they speak out against all mankind especially at birthdays. This should not be taken lightly and shrugged off as not important. The 12 Zodiac signs rule over people much more than they realize. No witch, wizard or occultic person can do you harm unless they use Astrology and your birth date. They have to be divinely silenced, made deaf and dumb to get your deliverance and maintain it.

It is hoped that all these factors would be taken into consideration as the Body of Christ learns to take territory and move ahead with God's End Time Army of Worshippers.

CHAPTER THIRTEEN

Let us Praise and Worship from the Heavenlies

Our position and posture in worship necessitates an understanding of the hierarchical structure of the heavenlies. Positionally on the physical, geographical plane we live on earth (The First Heaven) and look up to the sky where the sun, moon, planets and stars are as in the Second Heaven. Then above all that is the Third heaven where God's throne is. There is activity in all three heavens but whereas people have times of rest and sleep in the First Heaven, there is no sleep or rest in the Second or Third Heaven. Then whereas demons grow weak, tired and lose strength, the Everlasting God fainteth not neither does He grow weary and the God of Jacob never slumbers nor sleep.

We naturally feel at a disadvantage when we have to look up to the Second Heaven thinking satan is above us. Actually he is under our feet. This leaves the principalities and powers in the air. We are seated with Christ Jesus above them in ranking according to hierarchical structure. Clothed in heavenly armor we'll enter the land. We ascend in worship and descend in warfare according to Chuck Pierce in his book ---The Worship Warrior. The renewing of the mind is very necessary to conceptualize our position and posture. We think for example that humility is to be down at the bottom but in God's eyes that is the highest rank. Therefore as we humble ourselves the higher in rank we become and the higher our praise ascends unhindered to God's throne.

There is an awesome release of spiritual atomic power as the purified, sanctified people of God worship from this plane in the heavenlies. There is an unusual corporate anointing that helps us to move in the glory realms of the Lord Jesus Christ. Our very lives give off a sweet aroma as a perfume and fragrance of the Lord Jesus Christ as we bear His image and likeness. Imagine if you could, if all are fully clothed with this divine power how easy it would be to shatter satan's magic and sorceries because we have the real original and authentic power.

We as the Body of Christ do not read satan's lies in the daily horoscope but a lot of times our moods and mental outlook are colored by the elements which he hijacks and perverts. A typical example is a thunderstorm with heavy rain and lightning. Automatically most people enter into a gloomy mood in line with the weather. They feel dissipated and lack luster. Their energy, enthusiasm and motivation seem to take a downward slide. When the sun comes out people feel bright and cheerful. We must take control of the elements when they get out of hand and command that they cease to carry out the orders of principalities and powers. God gives sun and rain in their due and right seasons. Sudden and unexpected changes in weather patterns (although ordained to occur in the last days) need not take their full toll on the Body of Christ. We have to put all things under Christ feet---those things He has allowed to be so until His Return.

Father Time and satan's time clock must be held hostage by the Body of Christ. Think of all the programming that has still been done after the Resurrection of Christ. This has remained unchallenged to a large extent because of lack of knowledge by the Body of Christ. Jesus blotted out the handwriting of ordinances nailing it to His Cross so that we could reign and rule with Him effectively over the earth. We often hear scriptures quoted by believers—Oh God will restore the years that the palmer worm and canker worm ate out. But this cannot fully manifest unless the Body of Christ boldly use our authority to re-program the heavenlies and re-order our day. The Word of God declares the people that know their God shall be strong and do exploits (Daniel 11:32 KJV). The key words here are –know God—His ways and strong (this knowledge will give us the strength and boldness to engage the enemy's camp and take what belongs to us rightfully).

Rick Renner in his book"Dressed to Kill" devotes eight chapters explaining in detail how each part of the armor used effectively helps us to totally defeat our enemies with the might of the Lord -The implication here is literally what it states. We must be dressed to kill. The Helmet of Salvation underscores the need for knowledge not only for protection (we need the right knowledge to be protected in the head) We also need to know how to rightly apply that knowledge. Like the Apostle Paul we can say in these end times---"I come not to you in the wisdom of men's words but in demonstration of the kingdom of power". Isn't it instructive that God purposefully informs us in the Book of Malachi 4: 5 KJV that He will send the Spirit of Elijah before the Great and terrible Day of the Lord. Elijah had the power to shut and open the heavens thereby effectively impeding the idolatrous activities of the children of Israel. He reordered their day by force and for three years at that. They had three years of the absolute reign and rule of God. They had no rain, their crops suffered and they certainly went hungry. This power is the right of the believer.

It is also significant that a lot of heavenly activities will precede the Return of Christ. Most of this of course is catastrophic as the scriptures predict. However, before all this gets fully underway, the Body of Christ must blot out this programming so that "Now unto the intent to the principalities and powers might be made known the manifold wisdom of God "(Ephesians 3:10 KJV). The earth will witness the awesome authority the Sons of God which it was waiting and groaning for. When unbelievers cry out for help from earthquakes, thunderstorms and tsunamis the power of the prayers of the Body of Christ in demonstration can and will draw them in repentance to the Lord Jesus.

Let us Maintain the Flow of the Holy Spirit

He who began a good work in us is able to complete it until the Day of Christ Jesus (Philippians 1:6 KJV) God is a God of maintenance and completion of anything He has begun. He is the Self-Sustaining One and upholds all things by the power of His Word (Hebrews 1: 3 KJV) Every ground and territory the Body of Christ has taken must be maintained. Failing to do this allows the enemy to re-possess our land. This must never happen. Every territory that Joshua gained in his God given mandate to possess the land was marked with a signpost for future reference for example Joshua 1:9 KJV. He, like Moses reminded the people not to forget the Lord and His commandments, statutes and covenants. To do so would not auger well for their generations to come. Joshua and all the faithful Covenant Patriarchs carried out their assignments well.

We are a people of purpose and vision. We are also being perfected by trials until the Return of Christ Jesus. By a persistent endurance to trust and depend upon the Lord continually we will reap our reward if we faint not (Galatians 6:9 KJV) To withstand in these last days requires a fresh insight into the use of strategic spiritual weapons of warfare. We must re-program the heavenlies to be the overcomer of Revelation chapters 2 and 3. As Cindy Trimm rightfully points out in her book "Commanding Your Morning" we must do just that. Jesus's Ascension into heaven was unhindered because it was able to command that—"Lift up your heads O ye gates and be ye lifted up ye everlasting doors and the king of glory shall come in." His Blood and finished work had blotted out the handwriting of ordinances that was against us nailing it to his tree. He had free and triumphant access to the throne of His Father. The heavens were re-programmed in the spirit realm.

To see the manifestation of how Christ has reprogrammed the heavens for our benefit and glory we must ask the Lord to send His angels to take the BLOOD OF JESUS and the finished work of the Cross to each part of the Second heaven and blot out what the enemy has programmed into the heavenlies. Chuck Pierce in his CDS and DVDS on "Possessing the wealth of the Queen of Heaven" shows how we enter into our inheritance and all this enhances our understanding of worship and warfare in the heavenlies.

We must continue to reorder our days, months and years to become the Day of the Lord. God's authority is final and absolute. So must be the authority of the believers who make up the Body of Christ. John Eckhardt in his book "Prayers that rout Demons" lists vital prayer strategies for war in the heavenlies. We expect to be raptured at the Second coming of the Lord Jesus Christ (1 Thessalonians 4:16-18) We shall be changed into a glorious body (Philippians 3: 2) All of this requires being changed into His image and as a bride adorned in garments clean and bright we eagerly await this event. We are counseled from the Word of God to be found worthy to escape the Tribulation which will come upon the earth. This can only be accomplished by using our authority which must be based on strategic knowledge to re-program the heavenlies. This is because Jesus is coming back for a prepared people and an overcoming bride.

There is therefore a flow of the Holy Spirit to be maintained from glory to glory, from victory to victory and from dominion to dominion. Let us arise and get into this revelatory understanding of how to worship God in every aspect of His nature to defeat the works of all the principalities, powers and rulers of darkness. We will become just as he is in heaven it will be hard to tell the difference. The Head and His Body are unified and glorified together---One Lord, One God, One Body having all things under His feet.

As we unify and are transfigured into His likeness we cannot but maintain the flow of the Holy Spirit for the Spirit and the Bride say Come. And we the people of God the Body of Christ say---Ye lord Let it be so. We come to Thee Lord Jesus Christ. Amen.

Summary

In conclusion, it is hoped that the preceding research will bring a fresh perspective on how to withstand in worship and warfare in the Second Heaven as the Lord prepares His Bride (The Body Of Christ) to Usher In The New Millenium at His Return.

Bibliography

Baxter, Mary K. A Divine Revelation of the Spirit Realm. (New Kensington: Whitaker House2 000)

Buys, Amanda. The Four Elements. (Capetown: Product of Kanaan Ministries, 2003)

Cornwall, Judson. Worship As Jesus Taught It. (Tulsa: Victory House Inc,1987)

Eckhardt, John. Prayers That Rout Demons. (Lake Mary: Charisma House, 2008)

Hagee John. The Three Heavens. (

Jackson, John Paul. Needless Casualties Of War. (Fort Worth: Streams Publications, 2001)

Olukoya, David. Power Must Change Hands. (Lagos: Tracts and Publication Group, 2010)

Pierce, Chuck. Confronting The Queen Of Heaven. (

Pierce, Chuck. The Worship Warrior. (Ventura: Regal From Gospel Light Publishers, 2010)

Prince, Derek. Spiritual Warfare. (Wheaton: Tyndale House Publishers, 1984)

Renner, Rick. Dressed To Kill. (Tulsa: Teach All nations Press, 1991)

Timmons, J P. Mysterious Secrets Of The Dark Kingdom. (Manchaca: CCI Publishing,1991)

Trimm, Cindy Commanding Your Morning. (Lake Mary: Charisma House Book Group,2007)

Printed in the United States
By Bookmasters